DIRECTORS IN PERSPECTIVE

General Editor: C. D. Innes

Max Reinhardt

What characterizes modern theatre above all is continual stylistic innovation, in which theory and presentation have combined to create a wealth of new forms – naturalism, expressionism, epic theatre, etc. – in a way that has made directors the leading figures rather than dramatists. To a greater extent than is perhaps generally realised, it has been directors who have provided dramatic models for playwrights, though of course there are many different variations in this relationship. In some cases a dramatist's themes challenge a director to create new performance conditions (Stanislavski and Chekhov), or a dramatist turns director to formulate an appropriate style for his work (Brecht); alternatively a director writes plays to correspond with his theory (Artaud), or creates communal scripts out of exploratory work with actors (Chaikin, Grotowski). Some directors are identified with a single theory (Craig), others gave definitive shape to a range of styles (Reinhardt); the work of some has an ideological basis (Stein), while others work more pragmatically (Bergman).

Generally speaking, those directors who have contributed to what is distinctly "modern" in today's theatre stand in much the same relationship to the dramatic texts they work with, as composers do to librettists in opera. However, since theatrical performance is the most ephemeral of the arts and the only easily reproducible element is the text, critical attention has tended to focus on the playwright. This series is designed to redress the balance by providing an overview of selected directors' stage work: those who helped to formulate modern theories of drama. Their key productions have been reconstructed from promptbooks, reviews, scene-designs, photographs, diaries, correspondence and – where these productions are contemporary – documented by first-hand description, interviews with the director, etc. Apart from its intrinsic interest, this record allows a critical perspective, testing ideas against practical problems and achievements. In each case, too, the director's work is set in context by indicating the source of his ideas and their influence, the organization of his acting company and his relationship to the theatrical or political establishment, so as to bring out wider issues: the way theatre both reflects and influences assumptions about the nature of man and his social role.

C. D. Innes

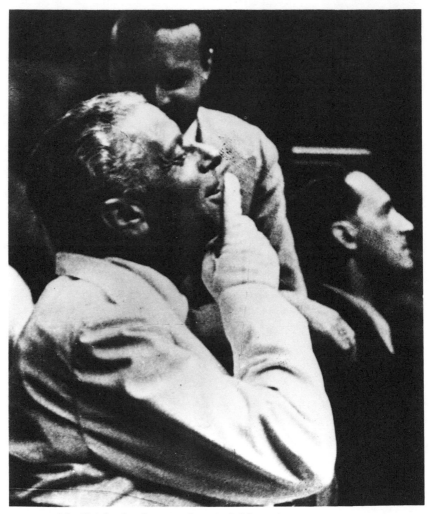

Max Reinhardt rehearsing *Faust* in Salzburg, in 1933.

Max Reinhardt

J. L. STYAN

Franklyn Bliss Snyder Professor of English Literature
Northwestern University

CAMBRIDGE UNIVERSITY PRESS

CAMBRIDGE
LONDON   NEW YORK   NEW ROCHELLE
MELBOURNE   SYDNEY

Published by the Press Syndicate of the University of Cambridge
The Pitt Building, Trumpington Street, Cambridge CB2 1RP
32 East 57th Street, New York, NY 10022, USA
296 Beaconsfield Parade, Middle Park, Melbourne 3206, Australia

First published 1982

Printed in United States of America

Library of Congress catalogue card number: 81–18172

British Library Cataloguing in Publication Data

Styan, J.L.
Max Reinhardt. – (Directors in perspective)
1. Reinhardt, Max – Criticism and interpretation
I. Title   II. Series
792'.0233'0924   PN2658.R4
ISBN 0 521 22444 6 hard covers
ISBN 0 521 29504 1 paper back

Contents

Illustrations

Preface

This is not a biography of Max Reinhardt, but a short account of his contribution to the modern theatre. Oliver M. Sayler's excellent collection of papers by those who knew Reinhardt personally, *Max Reinhardt and His Theatre,* was published by Brentano's of New York as long ago as 1924, nearly twenty years before his death and before the years of the main Salzburg festivals and the period of his exile in the United States. A number of well-illustrated studies have been published more recently in German, but there is a need for an up-to-date account in English which will look at the whole of Reinhardt's career in the light of our knowledge of the modern theatre and drama.

I am indebted to the Research Committee of Northwestern University for their support, to the librarians of the British Library and its Newspaper Collection at Colindale, to Marion Hanscom, Head of Special Collections at the Glenn G. Bartle Library of the State University of New York at Binghamton, and to Michael Jasenas and Marianne Janauer, Curator and Archivist of the Max Reinhardt Archive there, with its unique collection of Reinhardt *Regiebücher,* his library and papers.

The illustrations in this book appear by kind permission of the Binghamton Archive, and in acknowledging its help my thanks are extended also to the Max-Reinhardt-Forschungsstätte in Salzburg and to its director, Gisela Prossnitz.

J.L.S.

Chronology

1873   Born Max Goldmann, 9 September, in Baden, near Vienna. First of a family of six children.

1877   Family moves to Vienna.

1890   Acts under the name of Max Reinhardt for the first time.

1890–2   Takes acting lessons in the Sulkowsky Theater, Matzleinsdorf, under Maximilian Streben and Professor Emil Bürde.

1892–3   Actor at the Neues Volkstheater, Rudolfsheim, Vienna, under Pauline Löwe, and at the Pressburg summer theatre, Bratislava.

1893–4   Actor at the Stadttheater, Salzburg, his first full contract. Plays 49 parts, including several in Schiller.

1894   1 September, actor in the Deutsches Theater, Berlin, under Otto Brahm. Gains reputation as an actor of old men. Parts include Pastor Kittelhaus in Hauptmann's *The Weavers*, Tubal in *The Merchant of Venice* and the Secretary in Ibsen's *The Pillars of Society*. 1897: plays Foldal in Ibsen's *John Gabriel Borkman*. 1900: plays Engstrand in Ibsen's *Ghosts*.

1895–1901   Summer engagements in Dresden, Prague, Vienna, Budapest, etc.

1900   His first production as director: Ibsen's *Love's Comedy*.

1901   Starts his cabaret "Schall und Rauch" ("Sound and Smoke") in the Unter den Linden, Berlin.

1902   This becomes the Kleines Theater.

1903   Leaves Brahm and the Deutsches Theater; Brahm fines him 14,000 marks. Becomes director of the Kleines Theater and the Neues Theater on the Schiffbauerdamm: acts and directs. Joseph Ettlinger invites him to serve as adviser to the Neue Freie Volksbühne.

1905   His *Midsummer Night's Dream* at the Neues Theater acclaimed. His first use of the revolving stage. Becomes director of the Deutsches Theater. His first production there is Kleist's *Käthchen von Heilbronn*. Opens his school of acting at the Deutsches Theater.

1906   Buys the Deutsches Theater. Opens the Kammerspiele next door. The first production there is Ibsen's *Ghosts*, followed by the historic production of Wedekind's *Spring's Awakening*.

1907–8   Tours all Germany and Budapest each summer.

1908   Son Wolfgang born to actress Else Heims.

1909   Honoured with the title of "Professor."

1909–11   Summer engagements at the Künstler Theater, Munich.

1910–12   Becomes known throughout Europe: produces *Oedipus Rex* as his first arena production in the Munich Musikfesthalle and the Circus Schumann, Berlin; also in Vienna, St Petersburg, Moscow, Warsaw, Stockholm, Budapest, Brussels and London (at Covent Garden, with John Martin-Harvey).

1910   Marries Else Heims in Maidenhead, Kent.

1911   First production of *Everyman* at the Circus Schumann. First production of *The Miracle* at Olympia, London. First issue of the Deutsches Theater news sheet.

1912   First attempt at film-making: *The Miracle*. First productions in New York and Paris: *Sumurûn*.

1913   Son Gottfried born to Else Heims Reinhardt. More film-making: *Island of the Blest* and *Venetian Night* made in Italy.

1913–14   Shakespeare Festival at the Deutsches Theater: ten plays in four months.

1914   Wedekind Festival at the Kammerspiele, Wedekind directing: eight plays in six days.

1915   Visiting director in Stockholm and Christiana.

1915–18   Director of the Volksbühne in the Bülowplatz, Berlin, saving it from possible extinction during the war years: first production is Schiller's *The Robbers*.

1917   *Das junge Deutschland* (Young Germany) series opens with Sorge's *The Beggar* at the Deutsches Theater. Opens the Salzburg Municipal Playhouse. The actress Helene Thimig joins the ensemble. In the middle of the First World War his production record peaks at 48 in the 1916–17 season.

1918   Becomes director of the Kleines Schauspielhaus, Berlin: first production is Goethe's *Clavigo*. July: buys the castle of Leopoldskron, Salzburg (built in 1736).

1919   Opens the Grosses Schauspielhaus, Berlin (formerly the Circus Schumann): first production is Aeschylus' *Oresteia*.

1920   Initiates the Salzburg Festival with Richard Strauss, Bruno Walter and Hugo von Hofmannsthal: first production of *Everyman* in the Domplatz, the cathedral square. Gives up control of his theatres in Berlin and moves to Vienna.

1922   Opens the Redoutensaal of the Imperial Palace, Vienna, as a theatre: first production is Goethe's *Clavigo*.

1923 First production at the Schloss Leopoldskron: Molière's *The Imaginary Invalid.*

1924 *The Miracle* is his first production in America, at the Century Theatre, New York. Production tours the United States. Becomes director of the Theater in der Josefstadt, Vienna: first production is Goldoni's *The Servant of Two Masters.* Opens the Komödie in the Kurfürstendamm, Berlin: first production is also *The Servant of Two Masters.* Again becomes director of the Deutsches Theater: first production is Shaw's *Saint Joan,* with Elisabeth Bergner.

1925 Opens the Salzburg Festspielhaus: first production is Hofmannsthal's *The Salzburg Great Theatre of the World,* revived from 1922.

1926 Visits the United States. Discusses film directing in Hollywood.

1927–8 The ensemble plays in New York: eight productions in German.

1928 Becomes director of the Berliner Theater: first production is *Romeo and Juliet.* Lectures at Columbia University: "On the Actor." The Max Reinhardt Seminar founded in Schönbrunn, Vienna.

1929 Becomes director of his Berlin theatres again. Brother Edmund dies. Hofmannsthal dies.

1930 Twenty-fifth anniversary as director of the Deutsches Theater. Honorary degrees from Frankfurt-on-Main and Kiel Universities.

1931 Seeks divorce from Else Heims. Becomes vice-president of the Shakespeare Association.

1932 The ensemble visits London and Manchester.

1933 Outdoor productions of *A Midsummer Night's Dream* in Florence and Oxford. Forced by the Nazi government to give his theatres in Germany to "the German people": writes an open letter to Goering and Goebbels.

1934 Gives up direction of the Theater in der Josefstadt. Signs contract with Warner Brothers. Directs *A Midsummer Night's Dream* in Hollywood, San Francisco, Berkeley and Chicago.

1935 His film of *A Midsummer Night's Dream* for Warner Brothers opens in New York and London. Lectures at the Writers' Club, New York. Divorce finalized; marriage to Helene Thimig official.

1937 Last production in Vienna. Emigrates to the United States; Helene Thimig follows.

1938 Austria occupied by Germany: his property confiscated.

Opens the Max Reinhardt Workshop for Stage, Screen and Radio in Hollywood.

1940   Takes United States citizenship.

1943   Last production is Irwin Shaw's *Sons and Soldiers* at the Morosco Theatre, New York. Suffers stroke and dies in the Gladstone Hotel, New York, on 31 October.

1 An explosion of ideas in the theatre

Max Reinhardt arrived on the scene at the moment when the modern theatre was exploding with ideas and anxious to try new forms and styles of performance of every kind. The theories of Zola and Wagner, Strindberg and Appia contended for the attention of every theatre artist, and none could be wholly ignored. The physical playhouse was also at a point of special development, and there was a ferment of ideas about its best shape and size, and about the uses of the new electric light and the advance in scenic possibilities that came with it. Following Wagner, Reinhardt saw that the theatre could be the common ground for all the arts, and the writer and critic Hermann Bahr went so far as to claim that it was Reinhardt who "ended for this generation in Germany the sway of the literary play."[1] It was Reinhardt's privilege to put into practice some of the thinking of the "aesthetic drama" movement which wanted to combine the arts of space and light, of music, design and the spoken word, and of acting, mime and dance. His invention of the *Regiebuch* as a master promptbook was both a monument to his work – and a necessity if that work was to be carried out.

The Max Reinhardt who captured the attention of non-German-speaking audiences when his productions found their way outside Germany and Austria–Hungary was the Max Reinhardt of the great Greek and Gothic spectacles. For those audiences he was the Herr Professor, the master. There probably never has been a more magnificent group of productions than his *Oedipus,* his *Everyman* and his *Miracle.* The technical resourcefulness displayed in these offerings, not least in shipping them from capital city to capital city, dazzled the critics who knew nothing of his more intimate and experimental work at home, work which nevertheless absorbed most of his time and continued undiminished to his death. Broadcasting on the B.B.C., the British director W. Bridges-Adams said that the shows he took to England "were in the category that the Germans call *Kolossal*. Yet in his own strong way he could be as delicate as he pleased."[2] Allan Jackson of the Ohio State University Theatre Research Institute believed that English-speaking countries have a distorted image of his work: "His reputation is for spectacle when it should be for innovation and experimentation."[3] And this has been corrobo-

1

rated by his actors. Gerda Redlich said in an interview, "In England Reinhardt is only known through the *World Theatre* [*The Salzburg Great Theatre of the World*] and *Miracle* and that sort of thing, and that – that wasn't his strength: chamber theatre, small detailed, subtle work with actors – that was his real strength. And he was a fantastic teacher."[4] Robert Ryan, one of his Hollywood Workshop graduates, recently pointed out that *The Miracle* and *Everyman* were by no means the master's favourite productions.[5]

And Reinhardt had his detractors. Even in his own country he was accused of creating only spectacles, of being a mere technician with no true artistic philosophy. As early as 1905, following the celebrated productions of *A Midsummer Night's Dream* and Kleist's *Käthchen von Heilbronn* in Berlin, the cry was heard that he was only a stage decorator, even when it was clear that he was suiting the visual style to the content of the play. Herbert Ihering of the *Berliner Börsenkurier* was among those who did not tire of putting him down: "When at the turn of the century Max Reinhardt brought back the classics, what prospects lay before us? Did he put us into touch with their essentials? Did he try to open up a discussion on the problems of drama? Reinhardt and his times put us into touch only with production."[6] Reinhardt's visual achievements have been blamed on an over-subsidized theatre, and on his desire to please a bourgeois audience. Because he tried to widen the range of the stage after the narrow effects of naturalism, he has been charged with the catch-all sin of "neo-romanticism." And the American scholar Sheldon Cheney decided to brand him with a greater sin, that of making his method of production more obtrusive than the theme and intention of the author: "When Max Reinhardt 'theatralizes' a play, he is likely to strain it out of all semblance to its original self," he said, and considered the *Oedipus Rex* to be a case in point – "startlingly effective, but hardly true to the spirit of the play."[7] Ihering's dry comment on this production was, "When Reinhardt's chorus was let loose, it was unanimously reported that several maidservants screamed and went into hysterics."[8]

Above all, because he was an eclectic director, he was accused of having no style of his own. His critics have followed Ihering in believing that he left no style, only productions; no company, only actors; and no theatre, only performances – altogether, no tradition which might have become the basis for future work. Now, even if this were true, it would be more fair to suggest that the reason why Reinhardt left no style was because he believed it his task to explore each and every style. His demand for teamwork from every actor in every performance implied a complete submission to the play itself, and his perfectionist concern to identify the right way for each play was at bottom an effective policy of letting the drama speak for itself. This study of his work will therefore focus on the range of different kinds of drama to which he devoted his talents.

For if Reinhardt had a special *virtue*, it was surely his eclecticism. He was, indeed, arguably the most versatile director the theatre has seen. We may readily identify the particular contributions of André Antoine, Otto Brahm or Konstantin Stanislavsky to the growth of stage realism, of Gordon Craig, Vsevolod Meyerhold or Jean-Louis Barrault to the development of an impressionist and symbolist stage, or of Erwin Piscator or Bertolt Brecht to the invention of epic theatre, but within the range of styles which embrace simultaneous elements of realism, symbolism and expressionism in their appropriate mixture for each play, Reinhardt stands alone. Nor is this eclecticism a vice, a blemish on the body theatrical, since the twentieth-century theatre would not have wished it otherwise at a time when the true strength of the drama was perceived as an international and pluralistic force. Perhaps today only a director of the stature of Peter Brook can cross national frontiers as easily as Reinhardt did in his own time, and perhaps only artists of such stature can lay claim to ridding the theatre of its inherent provincialism.

At the beginning of the century it would have been a considerable disservice to the surging forces of the new drama had Reinhardt been other than he was. The revolutionary "independent" theatres of Paris, Berlin, London and Moscow had made their breach in the defences of the established commercial theatre in the West, and the Théâtre-Libre, the Freie Bühne, Grein's Independent Theatre in London and the Moscow Art Theatre had freed the stage for their own darlings: Ibsen, Strindberg, Hauptmann, Shaw, Chekhov. No serious repertory could subsequently ignore these masters. But the liberating efforts of these new theatres would have been of little account had no one followed in order to take advantage of the territory gained. As it happened, Reinhardt turned away from the sordid excesses of the naturalistic movement, with its narrowing vision of human society and individual weakness, together with the restrictive requirement that the new techniques of the realistic actor look minutely at human behaviour, but he did so because he could not deny the theatre or its players their natural urge towards imaginative self-expression. The success of Reinhardt's production of *A Midsummer Night's Dream* at the outset of his career in 1905 was doubtless due to its exuberant theatricality, its sense of life and colour after a period of drab realism.

But this was not a retreat to the past, and he did not return to the ponderous and declamatory style of the nineteenth-century German stage. He showed that there could be a more supple, plastic, even natural approach to the performance of classical plays, not too unlike the flexibility that Brecht also called for a few years later when he also attacked the entrenched methods of the German stage.

[Reinhardt's constant search for the right playhouse for each play was part of this impulse.]We shall see that he learned from experience that the size and shape of the playhouse could control the purposes of the drama, and were essential considerations in every department of production. Over the years he made aesthetic distinctions between every kind of playhouse, in the beginning balancing the smaller Kleines Theater in the Unter den Linden against the larger Neues Theater on the Schiffbauerdamm, and shortly afterwards deliberately setting his little Kammerspiele against the larger Deutsches Theater. As he increasingly broke with the traditional limitations of the proscenium-arch theatre, he employed such vast arenas as the Circus Schumann in Berlin and Olympia in London, finally turning the Circus Schumann into his Grosses Schauspielhaus. But even this may be seen as a preparation for such outdoor work as he undertook in Salzburg's cathedral square or Florence's Boboli Gardens, or for the staging of *Faust* in Salzburg's Imperial Riding School or *The Merchant of Venice* on a Venetian canal. Within a generation he had tried out hitherto undreamed-of ways of putting on a play.

[By refusing to close any avenues the theatre of the twentieth century might take, Reinhardt assisted and inspired a generation of new directors, designers and actors faced with the confusing mixture of stylistic choices open to Western theatre in the early years. For a generation the professional theatre of Europe and the United States turned to the record of his achievements in order to see what could be done, and what had been done, in the presentation of a particular play, or period, or genre, and speculated on what he would do next. For during his twenty-eight years of influence over the Berlin theatres, a period of constant innovation in production styles, of repeated testing of promising devices like spotlighting, the cyclorama and the revolving stage, Reinhardt was never far from the centre of experiment, and his total versatility made him the automatic recourse for those who wished to learn their business.]Taking on the temporary job of assistant or of *Dramaturg* at the Deutsches Theater complex became something of a commonplace among youthful aspirants to a career in the theatre, and Reinhardt seemed never to refuse. As a result of his general policy and attitude towards the drama and the profession, he contributed to another phenomenon: not only in Berlin, but everywhere, serious playgoers began to perceive the work of the director, the *régisseur*, as opposed to that of the actor, as the major object of interest.

Paris and Vienna had been the twin centres of the European theatre in the seventeenth and eighteenth centuries, but since that time Paris had dictated the cultural trends and the terms of popular success for a century or more. It was the Austrian Max Reinhardt who made Berlin the new rival centre. The Deutsches Theater had been founded in 1884 to match the Comédie-Française in Paris and the Burgtheater in Vienna, and when Reinhardt took it over in 1905 it became the heart of an unrivalled complex of theatrical outlets large and small.

The statistical record may say something of his achievement. Where directors today hesitate about committing themselves to more than two or three productions a year, Reinhardt averaged almost twenty a year in his first twelve seasons as a director, with each play personally chosen, directed and supervised in minute detail. Nothing passed him by, from the design of the scenery to the planning of the printed programme. He worked himself harder than any of his subordinates, and his pace did not slacken during the war years, nor immediately after – his annual rate of production actually peaked at forty-eight in the season of 1916–17, in the middle of the First World War. The *Centennial Festschrift* published by the State University of New York at Binghamton in 1973 counted some 452 plays performed on 23,374 occasions between 1905 and 1930,[9] and in all Reinhardt was responsible for well over 500 new productions (see appendix). In another kind of count, he also demonstrated his skill as a theatre business manager by operating over thirty different theatres and companies in his lifetime.[10]

In the service of world drama, he did not close his mind. There was, indeed, hardly a period or genre of drama, the work of hardly a major playwright, that he did not embrace and master, from Greek tragedy and comedy, to medieval and Renaissance drama (notably Shakespeare and Calderón), to the court comedies of Molière and Goldoni, to the German classics of Goethe and Schiller and the naturalistic plays of Ibsen, Shaw and Hauptmann. However, there was almost no Racine and very little Chekhov: here there seems to have been a blind spot; or perhaps Reinhardt considered these playwrights idiosyncratic enough to be left to their native stages. In the modern period, he devoted himself as much to the symbolism of the now discredited Maeterlinck and to the symbolist verse drama of Hugo von Hofmannsthal as to the early expressionism of Georg Büchner and Frank Wedekind, to the dream plays of Strindberg and the writers of the Young Germany movement. Thereafter he enthusiastically took up any new playwright in whom he saw talent: Pirandello, Kaiser, Toller, Schnitzler, Thornton Wilder.

He was overtaken in the general advance of the modern German theatre, as it happened, by his more politically committed juniors, Erwin Piscator and Bertolt Brecht. Both of these men owed some of their training in the theatre to the time each spent as a Reinhardt *Dramaturg* in the Deutsches Theater, but unlike Reinhardt they shared a theatrical ethic appropriate to a less middle-class, more politically conscious, audience. Piscator was a Marxist who made it clear from the beginning that his intentions as a director were politically radical, and his productions were planned to raise issues for public discussion and to arouse public feeling against social injustice. As both playwright and director, Brecht also saw himself in a political role. *Drums in the Night,* his prize-winning second play, which Reinhardt watched in rehearsal and had put on in the Deutsches Theater after it had first been produced in Munich in 1922, was frankly political, telling the story of a prisoner of war back in Berlin at the time of the ex-servicemen's "Spartacist" uprising after the Armistice. In Brecht's later plays the social and political criticism was built into the structure of his drama, and increasingly dictated his actual methods of presentation and performance. It was understandable that, at a time of acute economic crisis for the Weimar Republic, the work of such committed younger men should eventually draw attention away from a more politically complacent Reinhardt.

Although Reinhardt was never a political animal, there were some few occasions when Reinhardt the artist found himself caught up in a politicized situation not of his own making. Before the First World War, Georg Fuchs, founder of the Munich Künstler Theater, wrote a Passion play and proposed that Reinhardt be invited to Potsdam, the old imperial residence not far from Berlin, in order to direct it. The proposal was promptly rejected, since, although Reinhardt was still only a young man working to build his reputation at the time, the Kaiser could not forgive his earlier connection with Otto Brahm's production of Hauptmann's *The Weavers,* the work that the Kaiser considered to be "dangerous socialistic propaganda."[11] Of more importance, when war broke out in 1914 Reinhardt shared the widespread sense of a new national unity in Germany, and no doubt also felt what many took to be Germany's patriotic mission to restore the world to spiritual health; at all events, together with ninety-two academics, artists and writers, he signed the famous manifesto of 1914 pledging support for the national war effort.

During the war itself, as we shall see, he lent his theatre, as well as his authority, to the aspiring young playwrights who formed the society of *Das junge Deutschland* (Young Germany). These writers wrote expressionist "mission" drama, partly expressing their youthful individualism and idealism in the face of an authoritarian and conservative society, partly protesting the inequalities of sacrifice during the war. But we may agree with Ludwig Marcuse that "expressionist drama was only really political when it stopped being expressionistic and became propaganda."[12] At all events, Reinhardt soon dropped them, and after Georg Kaiser's *From Morn to Midnight* (1919) and Ernst Toller's *The Machine Wreckers* (1922), produced in the Grosses Schauspielhaus with Karl Heinz Martin directing, he had nothing to do with their more politically oriented work of the 1920s. When the Nazi party came to power, expressionist drama was banned outright as decadent and dangerous, and Reinhardt's theatres in Berlin were confiscated by the government. On 16 June 1933 he could do no more than write an ineffectual open letter of protest to Goering and Goebbels.

It is hard, nevertheless, to resist the impression that Reinhardt's eclecticism was held against him. As early as 1914 Sheldon Cheney was at once commending his "prodigious energy" and qualifying his praise by suggesting that Reinhardt "worked too fast to be the deep thinker and original creator that Craig is."[13] This was Edward Gordon Craig, the English actor and stage designer, whose record of practical work in the theatre was scanty by comparison. It is for us to balance against any such charge of shallowness Reinhardt's intense imaginative receptivity, to which everything theatrical was an unknown entity until tried out on the stage.

As a practical man of the theatre, Reinhardt appeared to know what he wanted instinctively, and his fellow artists came to trust his judgments. His talent contributed to the modern idea of the theatre director as a creative artist, a person capable of making final aesthetic decisions, and his work alone confirmed the possibility of having the single controlling intelligence that Craig pleaded for. It has been generally suggested that it was the nice combination of German discipline and Viennese sensitivity and humour which provided the right mixture for successful play production, but it is impossible to account for two other ingredients: his dramatic curiosity and his rare theatrical vision. For Reinhardt had the gift of dramatic perception, of recognizing exactly the right amalgam of the theatrical arts needed for a play – a capacity beyond literacy.

Reinhardt was a theatre man of so wide a range of relevant interests and skills that there is scarcely an area in which his touch was not felt. Alfred Brooks, first director of the Reinhardt Archive in Binghamton, believes that those in his debt included writers, critics, painters, designers, architects, composers, dancers, actors, directors and managers[14] – just about every worker in the theatre. He was ready to experiment with all forms of staging, from that of the intimate studio theatre to that of the vast arena, and with every dramatic form from intense realism to high stylization, so that his influence was felt everywhere in the West. As a result of contact with Reinhardt's work, Piscator in Berlin was quick to pursue new ways of staging and mixing the arts of the theatre, as were Harley Granville-Barker in London and Kenneth Macgowan, Robert Edmond Jones and Lee Simonson in New York.

For it had not been long before the German-speaking Berlin–Vienna axis of his work took in other parts of the old Austro–Hungarian empire, notably Prague and Budapest. By 1911 Reinhardt's empire included Stockholm and St Petersburg, and by 1912 he had invaded London and New York. His artistic and administrative abilities contributed substantially to the twentieth-century concept of drama as a world language, and to our sense that today the theatre is common property, ready to take its proper place alongside the non-verbal arts of painting and music.

However, unlike Stanislavsky and unlike Brecht, Reinhardt was a man of few words, whether in speaking or writing. He always had a strong disinclination to theorize about what he was doing. Instead, he let his work speak for him. "No one could be a better listener," wrote Hermann Bahr, "but he himself was a silent man."[15] Yet if he rarely committed himself in words, he believed in the immortality of the theatre and its power to offer its audiences an experience which could counter the emotional poverty of modern society. His belief in the theatre smacked a little of the evangelist, and was predicated on the need for community ritual. After the aimless years of much of nineteenth-century theatre, Reinhardt's legacy was to promote the ancient purposes of the drama – its shared expansion of feeling and understanding, its power to enlarge the imagination and intelligence, its gift of a special kind of delight to our lives.

Because Reinhardt made a great deal of money out of his many enterprises, some may consider his success to be more commercial than artistic. While it is true that he found the secret to satisfying the steady demand of big, middle-class, metropolitan audiences for sensation and excitement, as well as their constant desire for novelty, it is not enough to leave the matter there. The German tradition of theatre, especially in the Catholic south and west and in Austria, was always one of a spectacular religious drama which stemmed from the communal miracle and Passion plays of the sixteenth century, and Reinhardt's career in the theatre, even in sophisticated Berlin, repeatedly reminds us of a heritage he could not wholly reject, even had he wished to. When he eventually returned to Salzburg in order to initiate its outstanding series of festivals, choosing Hofmannsthal's version of *Everyman* for its simple strength and its universality of meaning and appeal, his action reflected an inborn sense of the larger purpose of the theatre as a community ritual. Nor from another point of view is this sense far removed from Reinhardt's more technical search over the years for a special actor–audience intimacy and rapport, whether by scale in his little Kammerspiele, or by the use of a thrust stage in his Grosses Schauspielhaus, its auditorium the size of a circus. Nor is it far removed from his search for a free and fluid style of performance, one in which the actor himself was the focus of attention and had charge of the house.

Roy Pascal has suggested that, after the challenging avant-garde plays of Brahm's Freie Bühne had undermined the work of the German court theatres, which had been the traditional source of light theatrical entertainment, the commercial theatre itself began to feel something of their cultural mission, and that Reinhardt sought to consolidate the new audience into a *"Gemeinde,"* a devoted community.[16] Cultivating your audience has been the never-ending determination of every company and manager since the theatre went commercial in the Renaissance, and Reinhardt was certainly a master-builder of audiences. The period before the First World War, when he was establishing his theatres in Berlin, is also marked by the development of new theatre periodicals. Christian Morgenstern's *Das Theater* became Reinhardt's house-journal for his two theatres, the Kleines Theater and the Neues Theater, in 1904; 1911 saw the publication of his own *Blätter des Deutschen Theaters*, edited by Felix Hollaender and Arthur Kahane; and arts supplements began to appear regularly in the newspapers, airing every new cultural topic. All this is evidence of the acquisition of a new role in society for the Berlin theatre, one which fell into a decline only when the Nazis came to power and Reinhardt retreated into Austria. As the earlier spirit of the theatre's cultural mission evaporated, the Grosses Schauspielhaus slid into the presentation of operettas and spectacular revues, and the government developed the theatre as its own medium for propaganda, even putting on open-air productions for the mass audiences that might have been Reinhardt's.

From the beginning of his career, Reinhardt's catholicity was apparent. In his first two years as a director (1902–3), cabaret sketches were mixed with the quasi-expressionism of early Strindberg and Wedekind, while the uncompromising naturalism of Gorky's *The Lower Depths* rubbed shoulders with rarefied plays like Wilde's *Salomé* and Maeterlinck's *Pelléas and Mélisande*, both prime pieces of the new symbolist drama. Reinhardt was no doubt juggling too many balls together, and it would be generous to suggest that he was searching for a set of principles. It is probably more true to say that he was responding with the eagerness of youth to the unusual variety of different kinds of play which any new director would have faced in the early years of the century. It was a time when the theatre in the West experienced a confluence of aesthetic forces, a time of great ferment and excitement, and it was Reinhardt's contribution to bring naturalism, symbolism and expressionism together and explore their possibilities. After Granville-Barker saw him in Berlin in 1910, he wrote to *The Times*, "One thing above all, the German Theatre has vitality; and vitality covers a multitude of artistic sins."[17] If there was a guiding principle among the few principles Reinhardt allowed himself, it was that "there is no one form of theatre which is the only true artistic form."[18]

In 1900, the year of Reinhardt's first attempt at production, the state of Western theatre was one of confusion of purpose and conflict of theory. The naturalistic movement, marked by Zola's *Thérèse Raquin* in 1867 and Ibsen's first play of social realism, *The Pillars of Society*, in 1877, was already past its peak. It had produced the kind of play which consciously rebelled against the popular romantic drama of the time, and the stage was now feeling a sense of release from the strait-jacket of strong emotions and moral sentiments, with its stereotypes of character, its declamatory speech and gesture, and an emblematic costume and setting. The naturalistic attack on the stagecraft of the commercial theatre, with the demands of the stock companies and the star system, served more than its own ends.

In matters of staging, the celebrated Saxe-Meiningen company had simultaneously shown Europe some of the possibilities of a more realistic stage image. From the Meiningen productions, developed under the control of one man, we also see the beginnings of the modern *régisseur*, a director who could co-ordinate every artistic detail of the enterprise. The planning stage of a production became of major importance, and rehearsals grew longer. A degree of realism was achieved which was the wonder of all who saw it, and a standard was set in ensemble performance which no new director could ignore. The realistic reformers – Ibsen, Archer, Antoine, Brahm, Stanislavsky – were all witness to what the Meiningers could achieve, and after their visit in 1874, the Berlin theatre had not remained the same.

The naturalistic movement owes much to Antoine and his Théâtre-Libre in Paris. This first modern laboratory theatre supplied a repertory of the new realism unmatched anywhere: Tolstoy's *The Power of Darkness*, Ibsen's *Ghosts*, Strindberg's *Miss Julie*, Hauptmann's *The Weavers*. Antoine also offered a first assault on the "classical" style of speech and acting long maintained by the Conservatoire of the Comédie-Française, a style which could never have served the peasants of Tolstoy and Hauptmann. But credit is also due to Otto Brahm, who followed Antoine by opening his Freie Bühne in Berlin in 1889, its first production significantly being Ibsen's *Ghosts* again. Brahm was the leading promoter of Zola's ideas in Germany, a scholarly advocate of "truth" in the theatre, both in its subject matter and in how this was presented. It was soon after Brahm was appointed director of the Deutsches Theater in 1894 that he saw the young Reinhardt acting and invited him to join the company, and it was through Brahm that Reinhardt first came to know his Ibsen and Strindberg. George Bernard Shaw was taken to be the leading British Ibsenite and naturalistic dramatist, and Reinhardt actually produced Shaw's *Candida* in Berlin before it was done in London.[19]

Nevertheless, Reinhardt resisted stepping into Brahm's shoes. Too much had been happening in the French and German theatre of quite another kind, and by 1900 a more attractive force had to be reckoned with, that of the new symbolist theatre. Drama has traditionally done a great deal more than reproduce real life on the stage, and the ancient theatre eschewed realism almost entirely in order to work on its audience symbolically and ritualistically, enlivening the imagination and touching the deepest feelings. At a time when some were pursuing the ends of naturalism with all the rigour at their command, others were searching for the visionary quality that had been sacrificed.

As it happened, Reinhardt had at his door the true source of symbolist aesthetic theory in the writings of the composer Richard Wagner, as well as impressive examples of his music-drama. Wagner's ideas about the art of the theatre, based upon what he conceived as the origin of theatre in the instinctive life of man, were highly infectious. It was for the modern stage to recreate the mixture of music and poetry, dance and song, with which people had expressed themselves in antiquity. The appeal in this kind of drama was not to the intellect, but to the senses and the feelings, and bringing together all the arts of performance on one stage was embodied in Wagner's thrilling concept of the *Gesamtkunstwerk*, the "total art-work."

Wagner's ideas about music-drama were heady stuff, and its leanings towards myth and mysticism attracted many disciples – Reinhardt has been claimed for one. However, in Wagner's time the techniques of the stage had advanced only to the point where his best efforts at Bayreuth seemed inadequate. It fell to others, notably to the designers Appia and Craig, but especially to a practical director like Reinhardt, to find ways of unifying the visual and aural arts of the theatre. Appia was particularly drawn to the notion of a theatre based on musical form, and, working in Dresden and Vienna, he set about revolutionizing scene design and stage lighting. He considered that the live actor looked wrong against painted scenery lit by foot and border lights, and he called for a free system of lighting from above, intended to project subtle tones and colours, and to render space and time on the stage more "fluid." The young Reinhardt cannot have done less than devour Appia's *Music and the Art of the Theatre*, and, later, the inspirational essays of Gordon Craig.[20]

Theories of a synaesthesia for the stage abounded, but to combine the arts in the service of drama on a day-to-day basis is nevertheless more easily said than done. Neither Appia nor Craig had much to show during their lifetimes. At best, as Reinhardt was to discover, one art tends to dominate another on the stage: good drama will make music a mere accompaniment, or music will drown the verbal detail of drama. Effects of light and sound are characteristically imprecise, resulting in a loose emotionality where none may have been intended. However, Reinhardt experimented repeatedly with the elusive ingredients of the "total art-work," and not without some success.

His rejection of the conventionally realistic stage and his search for new, expressive and emphatic ways of visual and aural, scenic and musical representation led him directly to experiment with ways of mixing the theatre arts. H. F. Garten believed this effort to be part of Reinhardt's neo-romantic heritage:

His heart was with the generation he had helped to victory, the neo-romantic and symbolist playwrights of the beginning of the century. Reinhardt brought to the sophisticated German capital a southern breeze, a dazzling display of colour, light, music, fantasy. For him the stage was not merely a faithful mirror of reality but a magic world radiating its own light.[21]

This is charming, but too simple. It would be more accurate to say that once Reinhardt had decided to abandon attempts at recreating an illusion of reality, changes in staging, style and emphasis in performance for which there was no precedent inevitably followed, especially with a man of his talents. He adopted every device he could press into use: he refined the techniques of the Duke of Saxe-Meiningen's company and its stage realism and manipulation of crowds, and made these a sensuous extension of the scene; he seized upon the opportunities lent by a cyclorama or a sky-dome to secure specially evocative and impressionistic effects of colour and light; and he perfected the use of a revolving stage to capture and control a deliberate pace and rhythm in a sequence of scenes.

Thus he turned readily to symbolist and expressionist plays where he could find them. He was particularly attracted to the kind of imaginative theatre which touched drama's frontiers with opera and ballet. And if he saw the chance of creating what might be called a "lyrical" stage, emphasizing the "musical" or "poetic" ingredients of a play, he took it. Possibly nothing of this might have come about without the initial inspiration of Wagner's grand conception fifty years before, but Reinhardt must take credit for managing the urgent, day-to-day reduction of theory to practice. He had to answer to his audiences.

At the turn of the century, writing for the stage was strongly influenced by the new symbolism. Ibsen himself had increasingly drawn indivisibly upon the traditions of both Zola and Wagner, and his later plays display no simple transition from realism to symbolism; rather, their special qualities stem from both. But another dramatist was seized upon as the new symbolist leader. It seems strange that Maurice Maeterlinck should have assumed the importance he did at the turn of the century – he excited the admiration of the playwrights Strindberg, Synge and Hauptmann, the composers Debussy and Sibelius, and the directors Lugné-Poe and Reinhardt. It seems that Maeterlinck's vapid poetry and medieval mysticism offered the new stagecraft of space and light just the simple opportunities it wanted. However, shadowy characters swimming in a twilight world did not long suffice.

Better opportunities were offered Reinhardt by his fellow Austrian Hugo von Hofmannsthal when he turned to writing his early "*lyrische Dramen.*" He called them "lyrical plays" because of their intention of fusing words and music, and in a number of explicatory essays he developed the idea that life and the stage shared the elements of dream. The economy of dreams was also appropriate to drama, and their impersonality supplied the broad sweep that a symbolist drama needed. For their mythical qualities, Hofmannsthal borrowed from Greek and medieval subjects, and Reinhardt was quick to lend support by producing *Electra* in 1904 and *Oedipus and the Sphinx* in 1906. The crowning achievements of symbolist theatre were Reinhardt's productions of Hofmannsthal's versions of *Everyman* and Calderón's *The Great Theatre of the World* for the Salzburg festivals in the 1920s.

Everything was grist for the avant-garde mill, and there could be no stopping the development of the sensuous stagecraft which had begun with Richard Wagner. But the earlier symbolist drama soon proved unacceptable to the more cynical and satirical stage of the twentieth century.

The more gristly element in Reinhardt's work came from yet a third, perhaps more subversive source, that of expressionism. The one quality common to all expressionist drama is its anti-realism, and it can range from a windy neo-romanticism to a violent dialectic. The expressionist always strove to put across an unashamedly personal vision of the world, subjective and often eccentric, and his method of doing this subverted the realistic objectivity which others held out as the ideal. His were plays of social or political protest, often of freedom against authority, and they were marked by a nightmarish mood and vivid colour and chiaroscuro in the setting and lighting. Sensational and tableau-like episodes were designed to appeal directly to the emotions, and characters were no longer required to represent individual people, nor the over-heated dialogue, often of rhapsodic and staccato verse, to sound like real speech.

Expressionism lent as much freedom to directors and designers as symbolism did. Unrestricted by realism, much of the drama was left unspoken and unseen, leaving a vacuum the creative artist was eager to fill. This was particularly true of the wild and feverish plays that belong to the youthful movement which gripped the German theatre in the 1910s and early 1920s, and the generation of directors which included Reinhardt, Jessner and Piscator owes a debt to the expressionistic release of theatrical ideas of that time. Reinhardt was especially involved with the idealistic Young Germany movement in Berlin, "*Das junge Deutschland*," but his thinking had been affected well before this by more important manifestations of the expressionist mode in the theatre.

Reinhardt was early attracted by three powerful forerunners of expressionism, Büchner, Wedekind and Strindberg, and before the First World War he had produced as many as a dozen expressionist or quasi-expressionist plays by the last two. Büchner, who had died in 1837, was not really reclaimed for drama until *Danton's Death* and *Woyzeck* were produced at the Residenz Theater, Munich, in 1913. Reinhardt took up *Danton's Death* in 1916, thereby establishing Büchner's place as a classic German playwright, although Reinhardt's *Woyzeck*, with its subversive treatment of the simple soldier, waited until after the war in 1921. Büchner had been interested in the kind of free stagecraft he found in Shakespeare, and since Reinhardt himself had acquired a close experience of Shakespeare in his Shakespeare Festival of 1913–14, the link with Büchner's expressionism assumes special importance.

Long before this the plays of Frank Wedekind had been the subject of intense debate: *Spring's Awakening* had been written in 1891 and *Earth Spirit*, the first of the "Lulu" plays, in 1895. Wedekind provocatively attacked the shams of bourgeois society, and introduced hitherto unthinkable subjects to the public stage. All this was very appealing to the younger generation, and Reinhardt's many productions of Wedekind's work gave the author vigorous publicity. In spite of his obvious limitations as a social philosopher, Wedekind's plays offered yet another opportunity to abandon the restrictions of realism, and his imaginative stage images were at once a challenge and a licence to producers to exploit the stage.

Nevertheless, it was Strindberg who was the most frequently performed modern dramatist in the German theatre just before the war, and Reinhardt was first among his supporters. Strindberg's personal discontents and the subjective perspective of his dream plays were strangely attractive to directors, even though the visionary action of his plays, with their innumerable scene changes, proved so difficult to stage. Reinhardt actually took his successful production of *A Dream Play* to Stockholm in 1921, but before this he had experimented extensively with many of the chamber plays in his Berlin Kleines Theater and Kammerspiele. Each of Strindberg's chamber plays assumed a musical form appropriate to its own tone and style, and attempted to dominate the theatre by a musical intensity of feeling.

It may or may not have been misguided for German writers and directors to seize on the Strindberg of the last plays as their mentor. In 1916 symbolism and expressionism would have seemed all one to the playgoing public. Reinhardt wisely threw out none of the competing modes of theatre. Instead, he worked with each of them, so that when he turned his attention to the classics of the theatre – Greek tragedy, Shakespeare, Goethe – he had a wealth of experience, and an arsenal of devices, at his disposal.

Reinhardt insisted that the medium for drama was man himself. The one element which Wagner, Ibsen and Strindberg shared was the actor, and Reinhardt conceived and worked out his productions, whatever their genre and style, through the medium of performance. He wrote in 1924, "Today and for all time, man must stand at the centre of the whole art of the theatre, man as actor."[22] And he went on to say that the theatre was at its best when director, writer, designer and composer had all imaginatively assumed the actor's part. By such thinking he acknowledged in practical terms that every play needed only that the actor find the style the play itself dictated. Thus, when Reinhardt turned to the classics of the theatre, he inclined towards the freedom of their more abstract stage, neglecting realistic scenery in order to give that direct access of actor to spectator he had known in the past. In his notes on Reinhardt's dream of a "Theatre of the Five Thousand," Arthur Kahane, Reinhardt's literary adviser at the Deutsches Theater, observed that "the really new is always strongly linked with the really old."[23]

The wonder is that, in spite of the range of plays he undertook to direct, "the distinguishing mark of a Reinhardt show," to cite Bridges-Adams again, "was the unfailing rightness of his choice,"[24] and in setting a new standard of production in Germany and throughout Europe, he did not antagonize the academic guardians of the classics or the even more formidable defenders of theatrical tradition. Reinhardt's was a bloodless revolution.

2   Beginnings in impressionistic realism

Reinhardt began his career in the theatre in 1890 as an actor, taking lessons for two years under Maximilian Streben and Emil Bürde. In 1893 he secured a contract to play in the Salzburg Stadttheater. By the time he was selected by Otto Brahm to join his company at the Deutsches Theater in Berlin in February 1894, Reinhardt had played no less than forty-nine different characters in what was then taken to be the realistic vein. He was not yet twenty-one.

Reinhardt was short in stature, unsuited to playing young male leads, and so he found himself cast repeatedly for elderly "character" parts, often the villain's role. If not exactly repetitive in themselves, such parts must have thwarted his desire to exercise his talents, and suppressed his sense of imaginative theatre. They included, however, some challenges – in particular, several in Ibsen, the hypocrite Engstrand in *Ghosts*, the decayed clerk Foldal in *John Gabriel Borkman*, the politician Mortensgård in *Rosmersholm* and Old Ekdal in *The Wild Duck*; Hauptmann's starving peasant Baumert in *The Weavers*; Tolstoy's sick farmer Akim in *The Power of Darkness*; and the major part of the strange pilgrim Luka in Gorky's *The Lower Depths*. He modelled himself on the actor Josef Lewinsky of the Vienna Burgtheater, a noted character actor who set histrionic standards that were unrivalled in the German-speaking theatre of the time. But all this was mere imitation, as often as not of himself.

When Brahm took him to Berlin on a first two-year contract, Brahm was the leading avant-garde naturalistic producer in Germany, sworn enemy of the declamatory acting style of the commercial theatre. Under Brahm, the young Reinhardt was able to witness a quality of realistic production he had not known before. Brahm insisted that his actor act, not just with his voice and gestures, but with his whole body. He was expected to perform as if unconscious of the presence of the audience, with no posturing, no playing for effect, no making of "points" and no pauses for applause. Like Antoine's actor, he might even find himself playing with his back to the audience. And each actor, even if only with a walk-on part, had to play in character all the time and seem to be interested when someone else was speaking, so that the whole stage was constantly alive. Every prop or piece of furniture had to be as authentic as possible, and every detail of speech and movement, however small, had to be perfected to the point where an audience was convinced it was seeing the real thing. The production of *The Weavers,* in which a crowd of some forty supers appears in order to paint a picture of mass poverty, introduced Reinhardt to the careful crowd-work with which he would soon make his own special mark as a director.

But Brahm was also a very academic naturalist. He had been a scholar and a theatrical biographer – never an actor – before he took up dramatic criticism and the cause of naturalism, and he came to Ibsen through an intellectual's study of the theories of Georg Brandes. Brahm's contribution to the acceptance of Ibsen and Hauptmann in Germany must not be discounted, but he was not the director to handle the more imaginative and "presentational" drama of Shakespeare, Goethe and Strindberg. His attempt to produce Sophocles' *Antigone* with a royal palace that was made to look lived in, and a chorus of Theban noblemen who roamed the set as if they felt at home, was a disastrous contradiction between style and content. His ideal of realistic theatre seemed no more than that of the photographer, and the sordid side of the plays he chose and their drab décor depressed Reinhardt with his Viennese temperament. He grew tired of "sticking on a beard and eating noodles and sauerkraut on stage every night" – which was the way H. I. Pilikian characterized Brahm's more deadly realism.[1] When it came Reinhardt's turn to direct a naturalistic play, he would not exclude the imagination.

Reinhardt's discontent increased when he enjoyed a touch of independence in touring productions of Ibsen and Tolstoy to major cities like Dresden, Prague, Vienna and Budapest. At about this time he also tried his hand as a director, and the first production attributed to him is *Love's Comedy* in 1900, Ibsen's early attack in verse on the conventions of marriage. Reinhardt experienced an unmistakable taste of freedom in 1901, when he and a few friends from the company founded "Die Brille" ("The Spectacles") in a hotel in the Unter den Linden. This later became the midnight cabaret "Schall und Rauch" ("Sound and Smoke"), presenting satirical sketches, songs and dances, its attendants all dressed like pierrot. In its turn, "Schall und Rauch" developed into the Kleines Theater in 1902, and the next year Reinhardt left Brahm and the Deutsches Theater. He had to pay 14,000 marks for breach of contract.

The shape of Reinhardt's rebellion against too narrow a theatre showed itself immediately when he produced plays like *Salomé, Earth Spirit* and *Pelléas and Mélisande.* Then in January 1905 he mounted a production in totally non-realistic terms of Shakespeare's fantasy *A*

Midsummer Night's Dream; the rebellion was complete and the world took note. Nevertheless, he continued to present a great many naturalistic plays in his own way: *The Lower Depths* (1903), *Miss Julie* (1904), *Rosmersholm* (1905), *Ghosts* (1906), *Hedda Gabler* (1907). Later came Tolstoy's *The Living Corpse* in 1913 (known in America as *Redemption*), *A Doll's House* in 1917, *The Power of Darkness* in 1918, and Reinhardt continued to offer important realistic plays throughout his career. In all, *The Living Corpse* was performed 251 times, and his Ibsen performances totalled 306.[2]

After the artistic success of his *A Midsummer Night's Dream*, with its delicate creation of atmosphere and generally impressionistic treatment, Reinhardt would never again be quite satisfied with simple photographic naturalism. A test case was his production of Ibsen's *Ghosts*, the play in which he had played Engstrand for Emil Lessing at the Deutsches Theater in 1900. He chose this play with which to open his new Kammerspiele on 8 November 1906, the year after his *Dream* was acclaimed. He cast Agnes Sorma as Mrs Alving, his fellow Austrian Alexander Moissi as Oswald, Lucie Höflich as Regina, Friedrich Kayssler as Pastor Manders and himself as Engstrand again – all good realistic actors, but it was his intention to drop them into an unfamiliar and non-realistic setting. It was a dangerous thing to do, not only because the content of the play, with its suggestions of incest, free love, prostitution, venereal disease and the rest, was risk enough, but also because he appeared to be offering a criticism of the highly respected directors who had produced it before.

Ghosts had already acquired a unique international reputation, one that had grown since its first performances in Chicago in 1882 and Stockholm in 1883. Because of censorship, Germany had managed only a few private performances between 1886 and 1889: the police had always refused to license the play for public performance. Then Brahm had produced it to celebrate the opening of the Freie Bühne at the Lessing Theater, Berlin, in 1889, and it had been produced again by Emil Lessing at the Deutsches Theater. With its relentless joylessness and blank despair, the play had left a deep impression on the young Reinhardt, and now he risked the future of his new theatre with his decision to try out his own idea of how it might be produced to greater effect.

Reinhardt signalled his intention to be different when he took the step of bringing the Norwegian painter, Edvard Munch, to Berlin to help him design the set. Munch's haunted, heavily "psychological," early expressionist style of painting seemed right for the painfully suppressed emotions of Ibsen's play, the painter's violence of line and colour matching the playwright's intensity of content. One of Reinhardt's regular designers, Ernst Stern, noted in his diary that Reinhardt had shown him a Munch painting of a room in which the chief object was a large black-leather armchair. When Stern protested that there was not much else to indicate how the room was to be furnished, Reinhardt answered, "Maybe, but the heavy armchair tells you all you want to know. The dark colouring reflects the whole atmosphere of the drama. And then look at the walls: they're the colour of diseased gums. We must try to get that tone. It will put the actors in the right mood."[3] Behind that casual statement lies the principle of much of stage impressionism – small concern for clinical accuracy without first securing the right dramatic mood and atmosphere.

The heavy furniture lent a sickening sense of moral oppressiveness to the action, as did the everlasting rain which dominates the play.

1   Sketch by Edvard Munch for Ibsen's *Ghosts* at the Kammerspiele, Berlin in 1906.

Munch's designs were outstandingly atmospheric, and the critic Frank Washburn-Freund reported,

We had a scene that used outward forms only for the purpose of deepening the central mood of the play by the way in which it arranged its lines: vertical most of them, horizontals, and curves, repeating the play and clash of ideas, as it were, in a play and clash of lines. Symbolic also was the way in which the room, although it looked out on a fjord, was shut in like a prison by sharply pointed, threatening mountains, piercing and almost expelling the sky, and, with it, freedom and hope. Every line, every mass of space, height, width – all played their appointed parts in this relentless modern drama of fate, and the figures moving in it, almost as if driven by some unknown force, seemed to be placed there by fate itself. They were like necessary spots in the design of the whole scene, like an accent in a bar of music.[4]

This description of Reinhardt's symbolist prison of a room, with its figures moving within it like motifs in fate's own design, is of a scene far removed from the objectivity of the old naturalism. Reinhardt's play was a different creature.

It was a production of shadows, with the ghosts of the past, the ghosts of the mind, being suggested to the eyes, and in the last scene, Mrs Alving and Oswald, distraught mother and dying son, were enlarged to giant symbolic proportions when their shadows were thrown up on a wall by a hanging lamp. Such impressionism captured the interest of the critics, but that alone did not account for the success of the production. Reinhardt also offered a play of warm and sympathetic feelings, the emphasis placed upon Mrs Alving's human and particular suffering rather than on the action as a document of women's rights and social protest. Siegfried Jacobsohn saw both Brahm's and Reinhardt's production of this play, and decided that Brahm's *Ghosts* was suffocated by realism and the dull detail of actuality, while Reinhardt's production emerged as rich and profound, "from the heart to the heart." The new tone in Reinhardt's *Ghosts* was not at all scientific, but one of "Mutterschmerz," "a mother's grief," and clearly reflected, not the rebellion, but the humanity in Ibsen.[5]

No doubt the intimacy of the new Kammerspiele contributed to the overwhelming impact of the production. "Every detail counted," wrote Jacobsohn. "Every line seems to have been spoken as if for the first time. Every situation comes up fresh. Every pause has a meaning. Every actor is in the right place. Every nuance makes its maximum contribution. Nothing is out of place, nothing is there for its own sake." The shock of Oswald's terrible end, the surprise of seeing him as an imbecile, was so painstakingly prepared that it did not seem contrived, nor Ibsen's intention falsified. And Agnes Sorma's Mrs Alving was so finely detailed even to the tiny movements of her mouth and eyes, that, although she had a good mind and spirit, "her mind lay in her heart, and her spirit in her instinct."[6]

Reinhardt's naturalism had managed to bring together the play's realistic touches and a wider symbolism, and the realistic structure and content of the play could not have supported the kind of weight and profundity everyone now found there without the director's larger, symbolist conception. Symbolism in one form or another would soon reveal itself to be at the heart of Reinhardt's new sense of theatre.

3   Into symbolist drama

The characteristic style for which Reinhardt became well known in the early years at the Kleines Theater, the Neues Theater and the Kammerspiele was a happy marriage of realism and symbolism. The American designer Mordecai Gorelik took him for a true symbolist, one who succeeded in synthesizing the arts of the stage.[1] What, however, was unexpected was that the symbolist movement that had been rather precious in *fin de siècle* Paris took on a popular box-office appeal in pre-war Berlin. This development probably contributed to the opinion that Reinhardt was a theatrical jackdaw, a popularizer and a showman.

The Wagner aesthetic, with its ideal of a simultaneous appeal to all the senses through the medium of the theatre, absorbed Reinhardt's interest, as it did that of many others, and he seized his opportunity of reviving the union of the arts which the stage had last seen flourishing in the baroque theatre of the eighteenth century. After the restrictive verisimilitude of naturalism, for designers in particular an indulgence of colour and scene was an expression of youthful fervour and a new excitement, and they boldly set about recreating images of the past, as well as of the present, in everything from costumes and settings to furnishings and curtains.

As for the director, the Wagner aesthetic offered a notable freedom from the literary drama. To bring the arts together inevitably reduced the contribution to the whole made by words and the use of the speaking voice. Music, song and dance returned eagerly to the stage, and the pictorial arts assumed a new importance in relation to them. Space and rhythm, light and colour, now became the elements to be explored and mastered. If Wagner's ideas were not always practical, Reinhardt intended to teach himself how to present them to the general imagination, and where a theorist like Gordon Craig enthused on paper, Reinhardt would get on with the job.[2]

His principle for the new visual stage was one of impressionistic simplicity: a cut-out scene placed against a white cyclorama, a minimum of props, and the rest was for the actors to create. It was a principle he applied successfully to the staging of multi-scenic Shakespeare. In the production of *The Winter's Tale* at the Deutsches Theater, Craig's notions of spatial design were translated by Rein-

23

hardt's designer Emil Orlik into simple, suggestive sets, as when Leontes' palace had its grandeur suggested by its towering frame and the pastoral scenes in Bohemia were given childlike qualities. This is William Archer's report:

Almost all the scenes in Sicily were played in a perfectly simple yet impressive decoration – a mere suggestion, without any disturbing detail, of a lofty hall in the palace of Leontes. For the pastoral act in Bohemia, on the other hand, a delightful scene was designed, for all the world like a page from a child's picture book. The grass was bright green velvet, spangled with conventional flowers. A blossoming fruit-tree shadowed a toy-cottage; and in the background some quaint masts and pennons showed the proximity of the sea. The whole effect was charmingly fantastic and admirably in keeping with the action of the scene.[3]

The change into the symbolism of Perdita and Bohemia in act IV was a change delicately supported by the music of Engelbert Humperdinck, so that visual and aural stylization worked their magic together. It was still only 1906.

The principle for the symbolist actor complemented that of the visual stage. Perhaps provocatively, Reinhardt chose many plays which had to be performed with a large element of mime, so that the movement and gesture of the actors, especially in the mass, could convey dramatic meaning, while at the same time take the eye decoratively. Without adopting the disciplines of the ballet master, Reinhardt's use of his actors nevertheless aspired to the condition of dance. Cheney found this kind of production "a continuous enchantment of the senses," and considered the style typical of what he named "the aesthetic drama." This kind of theatre was marked by "totality of conception, the fidelity to a single mood of exotic richness; the play is not conceived in one mood, the setting in another, the lighting in another; line and mass blend with colour, colour with lighting, lighting with music, and music with story, the whole affording a single sensuous impression."[4] For his hungry American readers Cheney was providing an outline of the new symbolist theatre.

The symbolist style could also be quite operatic, and it was symptomatic that Reinhardt should take up a number of moody verse plays as soon as he had artistic control of the Kleines Theater and the Neues Theater. Typical of these were Wilde's *Salomé,* Maeterlinck's *Pelléas and Mélisande* and Hofmannsthal's *Electra.* These plays do not sound very different in tone, and they all attracted Reinhardt by their artistic licence to experiment with the rhythms of sound and movement. Incidentally, it was the success of Reinhardt's quasi-operatic productions that encouraged Richard Strauss to compose his own operas *Salomé* and *Electra.*⏋

Originally forbidden in London, *Salomé* in Berlin ran for over a hundred performances at the Kleines Theater. Salomé was played – and danced – by Tilla Durieux, and afterwards by Gertrud Eysoldt, and Herod was played by Ludwig Wüllner, and afterwards by Emanuel Reicher. The music was by Max Marschalk and Friedrich Bermann. But the production was chiefly memorable for the opportunity it lent the painter Lovis Corinth and the sculptor Max Kruse, who designed the exotic costumes and settings in period. The sultry atmosphere and mid-Eastern sensuality were captured in transparent draperies, and Reinhardt experimented with sky-blue silk against a high cyclorama, lit by the new Fortuny system of indirect lighting, together with a spotlight to create the effect of moonlight. If the space

2 Wilde's *Salomé* at the Kleines Theater, Berlin, in 1903, with Tilla Durieux as Salomé.

on the stage of the Kleines Theater was not as great as it might have been, Reinhardt declared in a letter to his assistant Bertold Held that the mood and atmosphere were nevertheless "intense and original."[5] This was as early as 1902.

Maeterlinck afterwards expressed his gratitude for what Reinhardt did to promote his work in Berlin: his had been "the only theatre which had the courage to bring out two or three of my plays which all the other stages were sure could not be materialized."[6] Reinhardt had attempted *Pelléas and Mélisande* and *Sister Beatrice* at the Neues Theater in 1903 and 1904, and *Aglavaine and Sélysette* at the Kammerspiele in 1907. "Materialized" is an apt word. *Pelléas and Mélisande* offered its designers Leo Impekoven and Lovis Corinth a field-day in medieval mysticism. A castle of dark, forbidding passages and corridors, a fantastic garden of flowers and ornamental fountains done in yellow and green, and dresses reminiscent of English pre-Raphaelite painting made up a stage of brilliantly suggestive colour and light effects. In lieu of any solidly realistic doors and doorways for *Aglavaine and Sélysette*, the stage was draped in rich purple curtains, which themselves provided all that was needed for exits and entrances.

Gertrud Eysoldt was Electra, Alexander Moissi Orestes and Rosa Bertens Clytemnestra in Hofmannsthal's play at the Kleines Theater in 1903. Design was again by Corinth and Kruse, who created a giant palace with walls like those of some monstrous prison. Under the influence of Maeterlinck's shadowy mysticism, the manner of this *Electra* was lyrical to the point of rhapsody, and Sophocles' controlled and dignified tragic heroine in Reinhardt's hands became a woman consumed by the passion of a prima donna: when Orestes kills Clytemnestra and Aegisthus, Eysoldt executed a savage dance of triumph and then collapsed – an effect unimaginable in Greek tragedy. But these were among the earliest attempts in the new style.

The celebrated *Sumurûn* of 1910 represents a peak in Reinhardt's early work in the symbolist vein: it was dramatic symbolism at its most dazzling and charming. This play began its life as a small-scale production at the Kammerspiele in April, and in May it visited Vienna. It was seen by Sir Oswald Stoll, who brought it to the London Coliseum for six weeks in January 1911. By January 1912, it had reached New York's Casino Theatre, where it caught the imagination of Kenneth Macgowan and Robert Edmond Jones, leaders of the new art movement in the American theatre. In the winter of 1912 and the summer of 1913 it returned to London at the Savoy Theatre, and thence it went to the Théâtre du Vaudeville in Paris. With each new opening, *Sumurûn* became more elaborate, more subtle. It was this production which first made Reinhardt and his premier designer Ernst Stern known outside the German-speaking theatre.

For the play itself was virtually wordless, and its currency in pantomime, music and dance was international. The "book" was by Friedrich Freksa, but the story was told as much by Felix Hollaender's music. It had a brief spoken prologue in which the carpet-seller Nur-al-Din (first played by Alexander Moissi) squatted cross-legged before the curtain and announced that he was in love with the favourite wife of the old Sheik. The subsequent story of the play was his dream, and as a story it was pretty thin. Nur-al-Din's love for the almond-eyed Sumurûn began when he saw her dainty foot in an oriental bazaar – it was all he could see of the otherwise veiled lady. The Sheik himself steals a beautiful dancing girl (Leopoldine Konstantin) from the hunchbacked juggler's booth next door. The Hunchback promptly tries to kill himself, and his servants, afraid that they may be accused of his murder, hide the body in the very basket in which Nur-al-Din is smuggling himself into the palace harem. Once inside the palace, the Hunchback recovers and strangles the Dancing Girl, while in another room Nur-al-Din lies blissfully in Sumurûn's arms.

Recreated from *The Arabian Nights*, *Sumurûn* was given a highly imaginative treatment. As a child, Stern had lived in Turkish Romania, and for his designs he recalled the oriental customs and dresses he had known:

There were the beautifully dressed Turkish women who sold us *rahat*, or Turkish delight. And then there were Tzatza Frunsa and Tzatza Sciopa, who sold us fruit pickled in vinegar. I recalled them clearly, sitting cross-legged on broad divans before their low-roofed, blue-painted house. Their dark hair was bound in white muslin shawls and they wore wide violet-coloured *scurticas* lined with fox pelt, and their toe-nails and the soles of their feet were dyed a deep red. . . . In the bazaar there were fantastic Oriental eatables on sale, incredible sweetmeats and deep-black Mocha. There were dignified and turbaned Mullahs and Cadis to be seen, and, with a bit of luck, veiled women in flowing garments and harem trousers.[7]

All this Stern was able to carry into his picture of the bazaar in *Sumurûn*.

Nevertheless, Stern reported that it was done for next to nothing. He learned how to wind turbans for the men, and for the women he designed scanty silk drapes – fortunately, the fashion in Berlin that year was all for scarves:

Big squares of batisk silk in brown, black, blue or violet with irregular circles or squares were very popular as decorative neckwear. Out of four such scarves I made an exiguous costume for the honey-lipped ladies of *Sumurûn* – it was all they wore, and it received high praise as being both piquant and original. They went bare-footed and their only ornament consisted of wooden beads and ankle rings.[8]

This economy pleased the management very much indeed, and the only expensive costume was a sort of *bayadère* dress with a green jacket of metallic material, worn by the Dancing Girl.

Entrances were made along a ramp decorated with flowers, leading from the back of the house to the stage after the manner of the Japanese *kabuki* theatre. Meanwhile, the revolve smoothly turned the scenes, which changed from the frantic Eastern bazaar with its assorted booths, to the rose-coloured palace walls set against moonlit minarets, to the palace interior itself, a marvel of halls, galleries and winding stairs. Stern told the story of how, when the production reached the London Coliseum, Stoll had thought to please Reinhardt by decorating the stage with every colour of the rainbow. Reinhardt considered such motley to be the enemy of colour; he wanted a plain background against which his characters could move and dance in sharp silhouette. So, twelve hours before the opening, he had the whole set repainted white on a black floor, providing a flat, neutral background of great simplicity and no perspective. Stern concluded: "Every costume and every gesture was stressed to the utmost by the contrast. The so-called 'procession scene', in which the whole company defiled against a white wall, was particularly effective and it always produced long rolls of applause from delighted audiences."[9] The only scene painted in a colour other than white was that outside the palace walls, which were in pink, so that the eunuchs who stood guard over the doors would strike the eye with their faces and skulls painted green. This effect was thought to show a touch of decorative genius.

One or two indignant voices were raised against the idea of an old sheik in bed with a mercenary dancing girl, but otherwise London found *Sumurûn* "a thing of beauty, a joy to eye and mind."[10] Audiences were spellbound: "The like of this marvel has surely never been seen in London before! It presents harmonies of colours that are now suave and tender and now all ablaze and dazzling – the quiet hues of an old Persian rug and the glitter of gems; it has purity of outline and grace of movement."[11] If abstract painting, why not abstract

3 Freksa's *Sumurûn* at the Deutsches Theater, Berlin, in 1910, with Leopoldine Konstantin as the Dancing Girl and Spontelli as the Hunchback.

staging? The *Times* correspondent was so caught up with the spirit of the thing that he found himself writing his notice like a pastiche of *The Arabian Nights* itself.

As Nur-al-Din dreamed, Sumurûn passed that way, and by Allah (whose name be forever praised!) her eyes twinkled like stars through the faint mist of her veil. When they fell upon Nur-al-Din they grew soft, and she paused, straight and slender, like a palm-tree against the moon. Then of a sudden she fled like an antelope, avoiding the Sheik, her master, who stalked fiercely through the Bazaar, with bent brows and his beard in his breast and two scimitars jutting from his girdle.[12]

So the reviewer continued at length. No doubt it was the inventive series of living tableaux, the blatant sensuousness of the scene, the exotic invitation to the audience to let fly its romantic imagination, that impressed everyone. The power of miming, a glance of the eyes or a twist of the body, aided by the latest apparatus the modern theatre had invented, seemed to have injected a fertile new ingredient into the bloodstream of the drama. It remained to be seen to what good uses it could be put.

One other brief example in the pre-war symbolist manner will suggest the further possibilities of this mode. Karl Vollmoeller's ironically named *Venetianische Nacht* (*Venetian Night*) was another play without words, first produced at the Palace Theatre, London, in 1912. In spite of an entrancing performance by the beautiful Maria Carmi, it ran for only three weeks, possibly due to changes demanded by the Lord Chamberlain, who at first declined to issue a licence after seeing a dress rehearsal. There was no indecency in the play, but "the implications of one particular scene," probably one in which a married lady entertains a lover in a bedroom, alarmed the censor. However, *Venetian Night* rather lacked the vigour of *Sumurûn*, although it made up for it by having a special bite. Vollmoeller was another follower of Maeterlinck, and a symbolist with a particular bent for fantasy in mime, but this play demonstrated an unusual departure from the conventional misty mysticism.

The quaint, macabre story of the play belies its charming setting in the Venice of 1860. The scene is a small piazza, with a hotel behind and a shadowy canal and bridge encircling the left. On the bridge enters a blond German student named "The Stranger" in the appropriate Strindbergian fashion. He has a rucksack on his back and a copy of Goethe in his hand. He is luxuriating in the Venice he has always dreamed about, and at the same time reading what his beloved Goethe wrote about it. A gondola passes under the bridge carrying

Venezianishe nacht = Regie Max Reinhardt

4   Vollmoeller's *Venetian Night* at the Palace Theatre, London, in 1912, with Ernst Matray as Pipistrello.

an elderly English milord, his beautiful young wife, "The Bride," and a heap of luggage. On the opposite bank an Austrian cavalry officer exchanges glances with the unhappy lady, and she throws him a rose. The rose falls short, however, and lands on the open pages of Goethe. The student is transfigured.

The stage revolves and the scene changes to the hotel where the English couple is staying. Up a grand flight of stairs and along endless corridors, they are shown to their splendid quarters, while the student in his nightgown retires to his bed in an attic. With Goethe beside him and the rose on his pillow, he says his prayers and falls asleep to dream. At this point, a gauze screen drops between the actors and the spectators as if to mask off reality from dream.

In his dream, the student makes his way to the lady's room, where to his horror he finds the Austrian officer and promptly kills him. The lady tries to hide the body in the bed curtains, but such a thing cannot be left in the room, so the student takes it on his back and carries it painfully along a maze of dark corridors, down the stairs and out on to the bridge. All this as the stage revolves: continuity of action was wonderfully smooth on the Reinhardt revolve, and changes from outside to inside the hotel, and from room to room, were executed in an instant. When the student finally flings the corpse into the canal, bells are heard from the hotel and a porter runs out and drags it from the water.

It is then that the action of *Venetian Night* takes a bizarre, even an absurdist, turn. The porter fishes out, not one corpse, but six, one after another – all alike and in quick succession. With the sort of proliferation effect one might expect to see in Ionesco, soon there is a whole row of cavalry officers lined up on the bridge, each smoking a cigar. The porter in fact initiates a remarkable sequence of events, for as he took the bodies from the water, according to Bridges-Adams, "he tossed them high in the air and they landed on their toes, bouncing and quite dead. Still bouncing, they chased the student through the labyrinth of the hotel and out again on to the bridge, where, with a wild gesture, he threw himself over. But at that moment his bed came floating down the canal, and he dropped into it fast asleep."[13] Such symbolist–surrealist tricks were unique in 1912. Marinetti's Futurism was hardly known, Tzara's Dadaism emerged in 1916, Apollinaire's *The Breasts of Tiresias* and Cocteau's *Parade* were not produced until 1917 and Breton's first surrealist manifesto had to wait until 1924.

The notice in *The Times* found the unaccustomed juxtaposition of style and tone disconcerting. The mid-Victorian costumes and the multi-coloured decorations were delightful, with the women in chignons and crinolines and flounces, and the men in flowing pantaloons and foppish waistcoats. But this was all conventional, expected, making the shock of the subsequent action the greater. *The Times* complained, "Herr Friedrich Bermann's music, though often humorous, was at least sometimes ill-calculated. The hotel porters moved trunks to a delicate air, and the lovers made love to the blasts of a trombone."[14] We may wonder whether this effect was not well-calculated for its undercutting and ironic impact. However, the element of nightmarish farce in the scene of the multiple corpses pleased the writer. When the "regiment of facsimile corpses" appeared, the set was suddenly lit up and the stage began to revolve. According to *The Daily Telegraph,* this treatment of the action had the effect of "making a mock of its own illusions, and from room to room before our eyes the comic hero fled in burlesque agonies."[15] Reinhardt's game with the illusion of the stage was an experiment with the nature of the theatre, one to be seen as of unusual importance at that date.

4 Expressionist experiment

The expressionist impulse, that of an intensely subjective, all-exclusive perspective on a theme, was not new in this century. A dramatic form shaped by violently episodic, almost visionary, tableau-scenes had appeared uncertainly in the later nineteenth century, and at about the same time the work of Georg Büchner was rediscovered. Reinhardt was immediately attracted to the directorial licence afforded by expressionism, and turned readily to the plays of Frank Wedekind and August Strindberg that he found lying to hand. Reinhardt's gift of dramatic perception helped him decide what was worth salvaging from the mass of material written by these two prolific authors, each alike at one time forbidden the stage, and the fortunes of both of them owe a great deal to the promotion by Reinhardt and his Berlin theatres.

Without Reinhardt, it is difficult to imagine what might have become of Wedekind's career as a playwright. In his first sixteen years as a director, Reinhardt put on 1,171 performances of no less than twelve different plays by this controversial satirist. Of these, 657 were of *Frühlings Erwachen* (*Spring's Awakening,* written in 1891) and 350 of the more popular of the "Lulu" plays, *Die Büchse der Pandora* (*Pandora's Box,* 1904). Although Reinhardt had dared to produce the first Lulu play, *Erdgeist* (*Earth Spirit,* 1895), at the Kleines Theater in 1902, it was the 1906 production of *Spring's Awakening,* previously banned for fifteen years, that must be accounted an historic event in the growth of expressionism.

Reinhardt's first production of *Spring's Awakening* followed the production of *Ghosts* with which he opened the Kammerspiele in 1906, and it easily met the expectations of an audience looking for another innovative performance of a play with another challenging theme. If *Ghosts* hinted at a small catalogue of taboos, *Spring's Awakening* blatantly laid bare its "tragedy of childhood" to the public eye by showing the sexual awakening of adolescence. The grim subject was sexual repression, both social and psychological, and the pain of coming alive in youthful ignorance. It included the story of a young girl who dies from an enforced abortion without her understanding even how she could have become pregnant. It followed that from the outset the play had been damned as obscene. The scenes of prudery and bigotry on the part of parents and teachers were hardly taken for the satire intended, but as a moral outrage. The lyrical scene in act I in which the boy Melchior innocently meets the fourteen-year-old Wendla in the woods by chance was considered to be a sensational affront: Wedekind's original had Wendla begging the boy to whip her with a switch, which he did, adding blows with his fists until she screamed; Reinhardt's production softened this encounter so that it resulted only in a kiss, but even this shocked its audience.

By choosing a play which pulled no punches, Reinhardt subjected himself and his work to a trial of art against prejudice, and had to defend his author against police censorship. He wrote a spirited defence of the play's seriousness and value, as well as the importance of its new form for the development of drama and the theatre.[1] His letter to the police was nevertheless diplomatic. He first offered broad literary reasons why the play should be licensed, and then cited in support of his views a few impressive authorities, including Gerhart Hauptmann. He also pointed out that the play had been available in

5   Wedekind's *Spring's Awakening* at the Kammerspiele, Berlin, in 1906. Melchior is expelled from school, with Bernhard von Jacobi as Melchior and design by Karl Walser.

print for fifteen years, had run into several editions and had been universally well reviewed. Reinhardt then weakened his case somewhat by saying that the play would not in fact be reaching the public at large, since the designated theatre, the Kammerspiele, seated only 300 persons. Nor would many people be able to afford the high prices: the audience was built up chiefly by subscription. Such economic considerations, he added, were essential when it came to putting on a hitherto unproduced work.

However, at the heart of the letter lay a convincing appeal for attention to be paid to any new play of importance:

Here is the case of a writer already highly acclaimed and of great significance for contemporary drama, and of a work which strengthens and clarifies his literary expression and individuality. We believe that a theatre realizes its high artistic mission when it discovers a promising writer who is then enabled to say what lies deepest in his heart. We support him, moreover, for the sake of accepting the urgent artistic duty of performing a work of art which leaves the beaten track and suggests a new form of theatre that would be workable. So it is here. In this work it is not merely a question of new material, but also of an original form of psychological presentation, and the theme (the mental and physical struggle of adolescent youth) is approached with such moral seriousness, honesty, sense of value and tragic weight, is so far removed from the frivolous, so entirely free from ugly suggestion, that the chance of giving any offence to a sensitive viewer seems quite out of the question. In the long run, the stage may not neglect the serious themes that take us back so much to the tragedy of everyday life.

This was one of Reinhardt's rare statements of belief about the role of the theatre. He won his case for *Spring's Awakening,* and Wedekind's career itself owed much to the subsequent production.

Karl Walser was Reinhardt's designer, and he supplied delicately simplified, stylized sets. Alexander Moissi played the gentle Moritz, Bernhard von Jacobi was Melchior, Camilla Eibenschütz was Wendla and Wedekind himself was the Man in the Silk Hat, the "masked man" who speaks symbolically at the end of the play for the spirit of affirmation of life. But Reinhardt's role as a theatre manager in all this, his victory as an artist over the censorship, was possibly more significant than the content of the play itself, which today seems a little commonplace.

A comparable situation arose over *Pandora's Box.* Reinhardt had tried to produce this play in 1908, and at that time had written the police authorities another spirited defence, one which stressed the seriousness and "unsparing moral tendency" of the play's symbolism.[2] This time Reinhardt failed, and the play was not produced until 1918 at the Kleines Schauspielhaus, designed by Ernst Stern with

Werner Krauss as Schigolch and Lulu played by Gertud Eysoldt, who had played the character before in *Earth Spirit*. In such encounters between the stage and the community Reinhardt first tasted blood.

In expressionistic matters, the giant in the early years of the century was Strindberg, the mountain to scale. In the opinion of his son Gottfried, in his biographical memoir of his father, Reinhardt was "the Strindberg pioneer." His Berlin theatres put on 491 performances of the Swedish playwright, of which *The Dance of Death*, with Paul Wegener as the Captain and Gertrud Eysoldt as Alice, accounted for 100. However, this information gives no impression of the repeated attempts Reinhardt made to explore Strindberg's expressionistic *oeuvre*.

Reinhardt began his engagement with Strindberg very early, at the time of the "Schall und Rauch" in 1902, when he presented the more naturalistic one-act plays *The Stronger* and *The Bond*. He followed these at the Kleines Theater in the same year with *Intoxication* and

6   Wedekind's *Spring's Awakening* at the Kammerspiele, Berlin, in 1906.
The scene in the cemetery, with Alexander Moissi as Moritz and
Wedekind himself as the Masked Man.

7   Strindberg's *A Dream Play* at the Deutsches Theater, Berlin, in 1921,
with Helene Thimig as Indra's Daughter and design by Rudolph
Dworsky.

There Are Crimes and Crimes, and in 1904 *Miss Julie* was produced there also. The challenge was taken up again in 1912, when the more expressionistic *Dance of Death* was produced at the Deutsches Theater, and this was appropriately followed at the Kammerspiele by Strindberg's remarkable series of chamber plays: *The Storm* (designed by Gustav Knina with Albert Bassermann and Gertrud Eysoldt, 1913), *The Pelican* (designed by Ernst Stern with Rosa Bertens and Alexander Moissi as the mother and son, 1914), *The Ghost Sonata* (1916), *The Black Glove* (1918) and *After the Fire* (also known as *The Burnt House*, 1920). Others were *The Father* (1915), *Master Olof* (1916) and *Advent* (1919). Many of these, particularly *The Dance of Death* and *The Ghost Sonata*, toured everywhere in Europe, even in Sweden itself – Reinhardt's 1921 production of *A Dream Play* was actually first performed in the Royal Dramatic Theatre, Stockholm.[3] It was altogether an impressive service to render so demanding and elusive a playwright.

For Strindberg's chamber plays, Reinhardt usually conceived a strongly "atmospheric" presentation consisting of a rather gloomy set, with the stark effect of a spotlight picking out a character or a small group of characters, and permitting rapid changes of location. There would be a suggestion of chanted speech, and in *The Pelican* he introduced some extracts from Chopin to lend a supernatural air to the performance. *The Ghost Sonata*, designed by Gustav Knina for the Kammerspiele, with Paul Wegener as Hummel, Gertrud Eysoldt as the Mummy and Paul Hartmann as the Student, proved to be his most striking achievement in this vein.

As might have been expected, the critics devoted much of their space to giving an account of this most bizarre of Strindberg's plays, and not of the production itself, making wild parries at its meaning and its author's possible intentions. Siegfried Jacobsohn decided that the play revealed that "the world is a madhouse, a prison and a graveyard" and that "we all belong in one of the three."[4] But this critic also considered that the director was at least a match for the author, and perceived that the production was essentially musical in conception: if the effects of dissonance may be classified as music, then the nature and form of *The Ghost Sonata* could be attributed as much to the musical orchestration of the piece as to literature. Reinhardt's grip on the audience did not relax for a moment, and even in the intervals the sounds of an insane *danse macabre* sustained the ghostly mood.

The outstanding scene was that of the "ghost supper" in the second act. Jacobsohn compared this scene with opera, one with only one note, that of hate. The creatures sitting at the supper table were sinister, doomed, ash-coloured and strangely withering and fading away, like the figures in a ghastly waxworks museum. The performance was non-realistic, dim and misty – "like Maeterlinck," but nevertheless sufficiently solid and human to convey a frightening image on the edge of credibility, each of the guests at the ghost supper treated with a touch of grisly humour as they sat in their circle, the Colonel sitting stiffly with a patched-up dignity, the Mummy stirring restlessly in her chair, the Fiancée smiling fearfully.

For all the strangeness of the scene, Reinhardt anticipated every tone of voice, every nuance of feeling, in his customary way. Hummel started upon his long accusation of the guests in a deceptively friendly and conversational voice, smiling and looking round the circle as if for confirmation of what he was saying. Then his words began to take on "tremendous weight" until those round the table ceased to smile and sat stock-still in Strindberg's long silences. The harshness beneath the friendly tone grew more apparent, and as Hummel began to drum his fingers on the table faster and faster, then suddenly stopping, the tension became unbearable. As he felt his power, the old man seemed to swell, "sucking and drinking in their fear," until "the sweat of death stood on their foreheads." Through the silences the ticking of Strindberg's clock was heard, and Reinhardt had it strike eight or nine times while Hummel repeated threateningly, "It's time, it's time, it's time!" Finally he stood up abruptly and hit the table with his crutch, shouting, "I can strike too!" in a powerful voice, and completely losing his self-control.

At this, the guests all sat slumped in a state of collapse, all except the Mummy, who trembled with an inner excitement, got up and stopped the clock. In a completely changed voice, now quite human after making her parrot noises, she started to turn the tables on the old man and to accuse the accuser. As he was unmasked, he crumpled and dropped into his chair with a groan, choking hoarsely, and wincing and shrinking as if he was being struck. When the Mummy rang the bell on the table for the servant Bengtsson, the sound seemed to reverberate and be echoed by church bells far in the distance. The atmosphere on the stage acquired a sense of the supernatural. At this point the silent Milkmaid appeared fleetingly in the doorway, seen only by Hummel, repeating her "inexpressibly moving" gesture of drowning by lifting her arms above her head. The old man covered his face with trembling hands.

When Bengtsson took up the theme of unmasking, Reinhardt had him move round the table pouring tea. He offered the last cup to

Hummel, who himself began to make the noise of a parrot, and then of a cuckoo clock. As Bengtsson placed the death-screen before the closet door, as if following an irresistible compulsion Hummel got to his feet with difficulty and hobbled across the floor to the screen, where he hung, shrunken and dead, between his crutches. Then, with no will of his own, he went behind the screen.

So the guests at the ghost supper sat staring in front of them as an evening light shone outside the windows and the stage grew dark and shadowy. A harp was heard playing as the Student sang his last lines softly from the room beyond,

> I saw the sun. To me it seemed
> that I beheld the Hidden.
> Men must reap what they have sown;
> blest is he whose deeds are good.

The curtain fell slowly and Jacobsohn reported, "Strindberg would have been satisfied."

It has been well said that expressionist drama needs a midwife,[5] and the imaginative young director found expressionism attractive because it gave him unusual freedom for experiment in stage inter-pretation. When expressionism swept the experimental German stage in the 1910s, a number of leading directors were caught up in the fever – Leopold Jessner, Richard Fehling and Emil Pirchan, for example, but none more enthusiastically than Max Reinhardt. The movement known as *Das junge Deutschland* had sprung out of the First World War and its horrors. Promoted by Heinz Herald, at the time literary adviser to Reinhardt, the movement started as a private society in order to avoid censorship and to indulge a strong expres-sion of social and political criticism without hindrance. Needless to say, *Das junge Deutschland* and its activities were a far cry from the popular Reinhardt of *A Midsummer Night's Dream*.

In the two or three years of the movement, the number of Young German expressionist plays which were granted a hearing through the facilities of the Deutsches Theater complex was substantial: in 1917 (December) Reinhard Sorge's *The Beggar*; in 1918, Reinhard Goering's *A Sea Battle*, Walter Hasenclever's *The Son*, Franz Werfel's *The Visitor from Elysium*, Friedrich Koffka's *Cain* and Fritz von Unruh's *One Family*; in 1919, Rolf Lauckner's *The Fall of the Apostle Paul*, Else Lasker-Schüler's *The Wuppers* and Oskar Kokoschka's *The Burning Briar Bush*; and in 1920, Arnold Zweig's *Semael's Mission*. Reinhardt also encouraged other young expressionists by producing their plays, notably Georg Kaiser, whose first play of the *"Gas"* trilogy, *Die Kor-*

alle (*The Coral*) he produced at the Kammerspiele in 1918. This was followed by Kaiser's *Der Brand im Opernhaus* (*The Fire in the Opera House*) at the Kleines Schauspielhaus, and then at the Deutsches Theater itself in 1919 the play which was to bring him an international reputation, *Von Morgens bis Mitternachts* (*From Morn to Midnight*). *Europa* achieved a production in the Grosses Schauspielhaus in 1920.

Reinhard Sorge's semi-autobiographical play *Der Bettler* (*The Beggar*) was published in 1912, but had remained unproduced at the time of his death on the Western Front in 1916. It was something of a tribute to his memory when this play was chosen to begin the society's performances. Paul Wegener played the title part, that of the Poet, a Nietzschean superman, intended to represent the social consciousness of the world. In act II, he makes a grand symbolic gesture by poisoning his parents, who are presented as grotesque fig-

8   Sorge's *The Beggar* at the Deutsches Theater, Berlin, in 1917. Scene design by Ernst Stern.

ures of authority, science and materialism, before he proceeds on his mission of enlightening the masses and creating his Utopia. The play also includes the familiar angelic maiden, played by Helene Thimig, who loves and serves the Poet, and eventually bears him a child symbolic of eternal hope for the future of mankind. Crude as all this now seems, the play embodied the basic forms of expressionism, and surprised its audience with a rapid series of images, each a kind of *tableau vivant*, marked by changes from verse to prose and back again. Reinhardt was praised for having given Sorge's sketchy scenes a three-dimensional depth, and for showing understanding of, and feeling for, the new mode. In his biography, Gusti Adler, Reinhardt's secretary for twenty years, considered that his subject had not only responded to the violently changing times, when "all was in a flux, as in a bubbling volcano," but also found a method of representing expressionistic ideas on the stage: "Things happen simultaneously through a gauze, scenes glide into one another, as in the unforgettable coffee-house scene [in which the Poet proclaims his ideals to the world]. Voices, colours, dreamlike forms come and go. The theatre grows heavy with its destiny."[6]

In 1916, Reinhardt had placed a spotlight in the ceiling of the Kammerspiele above the middle of the stalls. Using only this spotlight and simple curtain arrangements, Reinhardt practised his clever scene changes with a magical rapidity in *The Beggar*, as in other plays of *Das junge Deutschland*. The Poet appeared and reappeared, now in front of the curtain, now in a café, now indoors, now out of doors, each stylized scene matching the subjective impulse behind the drama, the spotlight picking out white faces against a black curtain "like chalk ghosts." This phrase was used by Ashley Dukes,[7] who saw *The Beggar* in Cologne in 1919. Dukes explained how the fine gauze hung across the proscenium prevented the diffusion of light, so that as the spotlight moved from one part of the scene to another, the unlighted part was left invisible. However, Jacobsohn, reviewing *The Ghost Sonata*, found the same spotlight technique disturbing because the light could not illuminate the actors without also falling on the front rows of the audience, so "destroying the illusion."[8]

This complaint about "the loss of illusion" was not an uncommon one in these years, and whenever non-realistic staging was attempted. But the new lighting permitted the maximum flexibility of the stage and its suggestion of changing time and place. Ashley Dukes, indeed, felt that the expressionism he was watching was a new kind of poetic drama: "It never left the plane of poetry. The subject was modern yet timeless."[9]

Something of the colour symbolism of the French symbolists also appeared in Sorge's play, as well as the violent statements in colour of German expressionist painting – one thinks of Oskar Kokoschka's staccato style. The stage directions called for a heavy use of red, signifying madness: a red curtain hangs as a backcloth at one point, and the carpet is red like the cushions and tablecloth. Sorge had also studied his Strindberg for ways in which the subconscious mind could be realized on the stage, and he achieved a dreamlike mood by having nameless characters chant their lines rhythmically.

It was Reinhardt's lighting technique which best conveyed the Poet's "stream of consciousness" as it embraced one group of characters and then another, moving like the wandering mind itself. Walter Sokel has explained the effect:

When the latent substratum emerges, the centre of the stage is obscured while a particular corner – significantly supplied with couches or benches – is highlighted. When the mind shifts back to the surface plot, the corner sinks into darkness, while the centre is illuminated. The corner scenes, so puzzlingly unrelated to the main action centre-stage, can now be seen as only apparently unrelated. These scenes function as symbolically disguised commentary and reflection on the themes discussed in the centre, and in that lies their dreamlike quality.[10]

Each episode could be related to the central intelligence, and one part of the play balanced with another. Colour and light could bind the themes of an expressionist play like the rhythms and motifs of music.

The generally adopted style of acting for expressionist drama was also established in these productions of *Das junge Deutschland*, but contemporary descriptions of the actor's speech and movement are surprisingly hard to find. Picked out by his spotlight on a bare stage, and without the restraining support of realistic detail in a realistic situation, the chalk ghost began to assume the bizarre, even mechanical, qualities of an oversized marionette. Rudolf Frank described him as "stepping with primitive, abrupt gesture into the midst of the spectators."[11] The German actor's traditional flair for a pronounced theatrical manner may have accentuated the effect, and Gordon Craig's widely discussed concept of the actor as a super-puppet, an *"Über-Marionette"*, probably had something to do with the striking acting style which became associated with German expressionism.[12]

We may still observe the characteristic style in a few German films of the period, like Robert Wiener's *The Cabinet of Dr Caligari* (1919) and Karl Heinz Martin's film of Georg Kaiser's play *From Morn to Midnight* (1920). By analysing the latter in a useful essay,[13] Denis Calandra has attempted to recapture something of the so-called "ecstatic" style that evolved. It was intense and violent and very physical. The director Otto Falkenberg recalled a dress rehearsal for *The Ghost Sonata* in which Hummel and the Student were carried away by their excess of feeling and actually came to blows. The actor's body moved impulsively, and his speech came in quick and breathless gasps – possibly induced by the jerky rhythms of expressionist dialogue. Even when we allow for the idiosyncratic, highly energetic acting of Ernst Deutsch as the Cashier in *From Morn to Midnight* – as analysed by Calandra, with rolling and staring eyes, bared teeth and hands like claws – the actor is clearly exploring and perhaps defining a new style, one intended to match the explosive language common to the German expressionist plays.

The purpose behind such acting had little to do with reproducing the behaviour of real life; rather, it offered to project as vividly as possible a state of mind and spirit. Calandra quotes the actor Friedrich Kayssler, who in 1914 wrote, "It is the soul that plays the roles, not the body. The body is an instrument, loudspeaker, means of expression, tool."[14] In 1918 the playwright and critic Paul Kornfeld, a *Dramaturg* with Reinhardt at the time of *Das junge Deutschland*, contributed to the discussion a key essay, "Der beseelte und der psychologische Mensch" ("The inspired and the psychological being"),[15] in which he attempted to supply a philosophy for the new acting-style:

The actor must liberate himself from reality and be merely the representative of ideas, emotions and Fate. If he has to die on the stage he should not learn to die by going to a hospital, and if he has to play the part of a drunken man he must not visit a public house to see how it is done. He should dare to spread out his arms and at a particularly inspired passage speak out as he would never speak in real life. . . . He should not be ashamed to act, he should not disavow the theatre.[16]

And the Cambridge critic Richard Samuel offered a good summary of the style in a passage whose tone suffers a little from the ecstatic infection itself:

On the one hand the actor is but a masked and ghostlike figure, on the other a soul dissolved into ecstasy and vanishing into four-dimensional space. His speech is heightened to song and inarticulate shouts, or reduced to the weird eloquence of silence. His miming is plastic and his gestures are musical. When he cowers he is but a little heap of misery, but when he rises he assumes gigantic proportions. He is removed from reality whether he stands alone under the beams of the spotlight or amid the crowds surging around him. He is lost in the cosmos as the expression of the infinite longings of an ecstatic poet, the leader of a crowd in the intoxication of revolution or simply a member of a choric ensemble.[17]

Highly emotional, ranted and gestic speech is found everywhere in Sorge's *The Beggar,* and especially in the Poet's lines in act 1 when he "bursts abruptly" into verse to address both the stage audience and the real audience about his vision of the future: the verse form marks the central importance of the speech. Reinhardt at first moderated Sorge's high-flown style by containing the Poet's voice: he begins "vehemently, but not loudly" and with a touch of "bitterness"; as he gives an account of his tortured early life, he searches for his words "out of the depth" of his soul. Thereafter, as the Poet speaks of the better world all will share, Reinhardt's directions become increasingly powerful: the speaker is successively "elated," "more passionate," "filled with emotion," "possessed," "vehement" and finally "radiant" on the lines,

> Masses of workman will be swept
> By intimations of a higher life
> In mighty waves, for there they will see
> From smokestack and towering scaffold, from
> The daily danger of clamouring cogs arise
> Their souls, beauteous . . .

When the Poet's feelings soar, his voice rises and he lifts his head nobly. But Reinhardt also had an eye on the complete stage image, and he marked the development of the speech to its crisis by using Sorge's idealized expressionistic "Girl." She moved in unison with the Poet, focusing her attention on him and reflecting his emotion: "She rises involuntarily, more and more fascinated, moving up a step and staring at the speaker fixedly." When the Poet declares,

> Let woman excel in allegiance to man!
> Let his aim be: graciously to yield to her!

Reinhardt's promptbook note reads, *"Mädchen festgebannt",* "Girl transfixed."

At the end of this scene, the Poet speaks in verse again to make his final pronouncement. He first "rises slowly, stands still, runs a hand through his hair, lifts up his head and speaks quietly but with elation":

> You hurled a sky-high rock
> Upon my road –
> With rocks you cluttered, too, my brain, and
> I can barely think.
> Yet your hostile force steels all my pulses,
> O Destiny!
> One day I shall stretch up defiantly toward blue sun.
> An eagle,

I shall spread my wings
Toward the fires of the sun.
Talon and eagle! And your rock becomes a mote.[18]

For these lines he has "straightened himself defiantly," and "looking into the distance" speaks the last words with "assurance," "imposingly." Then, as he turns slowly away, the Girl "advances towards him, blocks his way, and lifts her arm as though to stop him," saying the ineffable line, "I must speak to you, wondrous stranger . . ." So the curtains closed. This was the ecstatic moment of expressionist drama, caught superbly in speech and gesture as well as in the noble composition of the scene, almost a tableau. Such sweeping sublimity involved, of course, the calculated risk of bathos, and must have called for a considerable degree of wise control and restraint in the performance.

Few of these passionate young plays left Germany. *From Morn to Midnight* was well received in New York when it was done by the Theatre Guild in 1922, and in London in 1925 Peter Godfrey presented it at his tiny Gate Theatre on the top floor of a ramshackle warehouse in a Covent Garden alley. Godfrey's production received enthusiastic notices, although much of the credit for promoting interest in the play must go to Ashley Dukes, who was both its translator and its warm advocate.[19] But Reinhardt was the true pioneer who found a valid method of staging such lyrical, free-wheeling plays, and showed how expressionism could be a suitable form for modern dramatic developments. The test had come in 1916, when he undertook a major play of both subtle feeling and incisive ideas, Büchner's quasi-expressionistic study of the French Revolution, *Dantons Tod* (*Danton's Death*).

A remarkable piece of modern theatrical history has been the belated discovery and success of the early nineteenth-century plays of Georg Büchner, who died at the age of twenty-three without having seen any of his work on the stage. Through his reading of Shakespeare, Büchner had alone invented a new stage idiom for a modern political drama, often vividly realistic in language, yet especially unusual in its use of episodic form. With each new juxtaposition of scene, a fresh perspective could be granted the subject of the play, and in this Shakespeare served as the link between Büchner and Brecht, and between Büchner and Reinhardt. Büchner's one comedy, *Leonce and Lena*, has political overtones, but it is his two masterpieces, the politically pessimistic *Danton's Death* and the pathetic satire on social injustice, *Woyzeck*, that were a hundred years ahead of their time. Both have affected the direction modern drama has taken, and Reinhardt produced both by the methods he had tested in the production of Shakespeare.

Mixing big public scenes with scenes of insight into the personal life and the mind of Danton, *Danton's Death* was a daring choice. Designed by Ernst Stern with Moissi as Danton, the production's long life began in 1916 at the Deutsches Theater, travelled exhaustively round Europe, returned to the Grosses Schauspielhaus in 1921 and with Paul Hartmann as Danton was finally shipped to the Century Theatre, New York, where, according to Brooks Atkinson of the *New York Times*,[20] the enthusiasm of the American audience was "unprecedented." In 1920 Reinhardt also tried the more melodramatic *Danton* of the Nobel Prize winner Romain Rolland at the Grosses Schauspielhaus, but soon reverted to Büchner's play.

Heinz Herald has explained how the production abandoned realistic scenery, and presented the visual aspects of the play "chiefly as human bodies and lighting effects." The set was therefore simple:

The stage was a neutral construction which was neither obviously interior nor exterior and therefore served as both. To the right and left of it great pillars reared up into the flies. The changing background of the play was represented very simply by various coloured hangings, and steps, on which the members of the Convention or of the Revolutionary Tribunal sat. At the same time these steps served to represent the front of the Palais de Justice up which the turbulent masses raced to storm the building. Here and there railings were used, a wall with bookshelves, a barred prison window. Perhaps two or three times throughout the play, not more, a sombre silhouette of old Paris appeared in the distance. All this would change, merge and disappear in a moment or two. What constantly remained were the two columns on either side of the stage, and they were constantly treated as an integral part of the play and drawn into the action. It was in this framework that the tragedy of Danton was allowed to unroll.[21]

Such a neutral setting permitted the insertion of variegated street scenes among the more formal political debates. Intimate moments between Danton and his wife Julie, or between deputy Camille Desmoulins and his wife Lucille, were set sharply against the more impersonal presentation of Robespierre and St Just. An "interior" scene like that of the bloodthirsty Tribunal could be carried over into the public square before the Palais de Justice by the continuity of voices and movement and, by control of pace and emphasis and tone in the playing, detached and apparently kaleidoscopic episodes were felt to be in rhythmic contrast. By mixing scenes of high life and low life, by mingling elegant rhetoric with drunken bawdy, the play pro-

Bühnenbild zu „Dantons Tod"

Ludwig Kainer

9 Büchner's *Danton's Death* at the Deutsches Theater, Berlin, in 1916.
Scene design by Ludwig Kainer.

jected a rich, three-dimensional picture of real life through the medium of its structure.

Again, it was the new use of focused lighting that also made all this possible, and enabled the stage to pass from one scene to another in rapid succession with unexpectedly ironic and satirical impact, as when a city scene of the Paris mob suddenly changed to show Danton in a tender moment with Julie, or to reveal him flirting with a whore. In his review, Jacobsohn considered that the key to the production was the darkness itself, the dark which "gives birth to light":

The light goes out, the columns or side pillars of the set appear in front of, or in the middle of, or behind a window or a lattice or a curtain, while already the noise of the next scene has begun – singing, drums, laughter, weeping, shouts. When the light comes on again, a bed, or a bookcase has been placed in front of the curtain; or an actor who is the spokesman for the Tribunal is standing between the pillars; or else a wooden platform for the prisoners, the guillotine and the basket in which their heads will lie. Overwhelming impressions coming one after another, five, ten, twenty times.[22]

By the speed of the changes the stage seemed to expand uncannily in depth and on both sides.

Reinhardt and Stern, perhaps impressed by Gordon Craig's use of shafts of light as a form of setting, decided that even the unfailing revolve could not cope with Büchner's frequent scene changes. They fell back upon lighting for the answer – "painting with light, stressing only the essentials" – and the result was unprecedented. Herald again provides one of the best descriptions of a Reinhardt effect, especially in the way it touched on another Reinhardt innovation, his use of a crowd:

The impression of tremendous plenitude and variety of life, the impression of passionate movement, was obtained by lighting up only one small part of the stage at a time whilst the rest remained in gloom. Only individuals or small groups were picked out in the spotlight whilst the masses always remained in semi-darkness, or even in complete darkness. But they were always there and they could be heard murmuring, speaking, shouting. Out of the darkness an upraised arm would catch the light, and in this way thousands seemed to be where hundreds were in fact.

The rapid play of light and darkness continued throughout the production:

Scenes would flash up for a second or two. Lights would go out, darkness would persist for a fraction, and then lights would go up elsewhere, and this rapid and often abrupt change reinforced the rhythm of the piece. The last words of one scene were still being spoken when the first words of the next would sound and the light change to it. The sound of singing, the whistling of "The Marseillaise," the tramping of many feet, booing, the echo of a speech being delivered somewhere, applause from out of the darkness. A lamp-post lights up and the mob is seen hanging an aristocrat. Half-naked furies in colourful rags dance "La Carmagnole."

It was against all this that the central story-line was maintained:

Already the light turns to a peaceful room in which Danton is resting in the arms of a *grisette*. And because whatever is the important thing for the moment is suddenly illuminated out of the darkness in a fiery or ghostly white light, the producer is able to stress the main figures of the play and their action to the utmost: Danton, the People's Tribune; the young Desmoulins; the sea-green Robespierre; St Just with the fair-haired, girlish head and the heart of ice – they appear for a moment or two and disappear again. And at the end the slim Lucille who has lost her Desmoulins leans exhausted against the guillotine. A short and deeply moving moment in the cold light of the moon.[23]

Reinhardt's crowd was well drilled, and by placing it downstage and in the balconies of the theatre, he induced a special response

from the audience wherever he took the play. In giving an eyewit-
ness account of Moissi as Danton, Wolfram Viehweg suggested how
the trick of sympathetic association worked:

Moissi, one might almost say, was a delicately built Danton, all lightness,
with a distant smile. He wore on his head a high, curly rococo wig. His
action and speech were soft and restrained until, in the great speech for the
defence before the Revolutionary Tribunal, he unleashed the whole force of
his temperament. At a guest performance in Basel on 3 June, 1917 the audience was so carried away by this scene that it joined with loud shouting and
hand-clapping in the stage-crowd's demonstration of sympathy and
approval.[24]

However, this effect was actually the peak of a series of crowd effects.
In the formal scenes of the National Convention and the Tribunal,
first a dignified, pedantic Robespierre was seen perched high on a
rostrum among the rows of deputies, and made a carefully calculated
speech to the precisely dovetailed applause of his audience:

They posture and they tremble. But I say to you, whoever trembles now is
guilty; innocence never trembled at the public care. (*Universal applause.*)

Then this excitement was itself aggravated by the more emotive words
of the icy, unctuous St Just:

Mankind shall emerge from this blood-bath like earth from the waters of the
deluge – with new giant's strength, with limbs born for the first time. (*Long,
uninterrupted applause. Several members rise enthusiastically.*)

Finally, Danton himself stood in the dock and attacked his accusers
with reason and sarcasm, his words lifting the mob to a pitch of
ecstasy:

Citizens, you need loaves; they can only fling you heads. Citizens, you are
thirsty; you lick blood from the planks of the guillotine! (*Tumult: cries of
applause.*)[25]

The speech ends with the shouts of the crowd, the ringing of Danton's laughter and rolls on the drums of the soldiers. The noise of
jeering and hooting was all around the respectable, middle-class
theatregoers sitting in the dark, and even in New York they found
themselves caught up in the fervour of the performance.

Danton's Death was not only a political spectacle, it also served
Reinhardt's talents well in providing a central character of considerable complexity and enough of a private life to appeal to the director's
more sensitive and subtle gifts.[26] It may not have been the sort of
play that Reinhardt most enjoyed producing, but it bore his mark as
a visionary director from start to finish.

5 Reinhardt's Shakespeare

Through all the years of Reinhardt's practice in realism, symbolism and expressionism he was also producing and applying these modes of performance to Shakespeare. It was through his Shakespeare productions that Reinhardt became nationally and internationally known, because he was among the first directors to approach the great plays with eyes unclouded by the traditional staging of the Victorian age. In his time Reinhardt produced twenty-two of the plays in the canon, and by 1930 he had presented 2,527 performances of plays by Shakespeare, more than twice the number of performances of plays by the next contender, Bernard Shaw, whose plays were performed 1,207 times.[1] In one season at the Deutsches Theater, that of 1913-14, Reinhardt offered new productions of no fewer than ten of Shakespeare's plays, and this Reinhardt Shakespeare Festival signalled a major revival of interest in Shakespearian drama in central Europe, with Berlin as important a centre for seeing Shakespeare as London itself. In a talk on acting given in 1930, Reinhardt declared his faith in the master in these terms: "Shakespeare is the greatest and the quite incomparable piece of good luck that has befallen the theatre. He was at once a poet, an actor and a director. He painted landscapes and built architectural structures with his words. He took the palm in everything he did. He created a complete and magical world."[2] Throughout his career, Reinhardt returned again and again to his favourite, often reviving plays he had attempted before. It was as if there were always more to discover, always more to realize, on the stage; it was as if the director needed to nourish himself and his art at the inexhaustible spring.

Reinhardt arrived at the moment when the idea of realism and "authenticity" in Shakespeare production, as consummately demonstrated according to contemporary standards by the Saxe-Meiningen company, was being seriously questioned for the first time. In Germany the early tradition of the "English comedians" was apparently not entirely forgotten – that of the strolling players who made a nomadic living in northern Europe after 1592 by presenting their entertainments, done with the minimum of props in pantomime and low German on a portable booth stage of Elizabethan conception. Nor was the indigenous tradition of the sixteenth-century Pas-

51

sion play quite dead, a popular spectacle using multiple scenes on an unlocalized stage. Starting in 1889, the director of the Munich Theatre Royal, Jocza Savits, revived the tradition of uncluttered Shakespeare by dividing his stage into three parts: an apron jutting from the proscenium frame into the auditorium, a neutral acting area in the centre and a changeable scenic background upstage. Without adopting the excesses of the so-called "Elizabethanism" which William Poel was practising at about the same time in London, Savits's way with Shakespeare was a comfortable compromise: using a designer's picture-book stage, retaining all the mechanics which Poel would have called the "ingenious toys" of the modern theatre, while emphasizing the Shakespearian actor's essential acting space, a large empty area in close proximity to the audience. Savits was working towards the kind of open-stage Shakespeare of the twentieth century, in which continuity in the action was achieved simply by having a minimum of scenery, a development we associate with the revolutionary productions of the comedies by Granville-Barker at the Savoy Theatre, London, in 1912 and 1914, and in the Tyrone Guthrie theatres after 1953. The new staging permitted the actor a more liberal stagecraft, helped him to get in touch with his audience and made it possible to recapture something of Shakespeare's own rhythms and style.

In spite of having at his disposal more of the sophisticated apparatus of modern theatrecraft than probably any other director of the time, Reinhardt's impulse was also to return to Elizabethan simplicity. Like Poel in England and Jacques Copeau in France, he saw nothing anachronistic in reverting to the imaginative freedom of an empty stage. In his pursuit of a more flexible Shakespearian idiom, Reinhardt soon shifted from a more conservative and realistic presentation to an increasingly undecorated style in which the playwright and not the scene designer, the actor and not the director, were central. Nor was he pedantic in this, but adapted his plans to meet the individual needs of each play. So it was that, in his constant experimentation at the Deutsches Theater, he established what many thought to be the characteristic style of Shakespearian performance for the twentieth century – free-flowing, highly rhythmic, leaning towards a symbolist use of colour and design, seeking the right visual images for each play's mood and atmosphere, and catching the most telling emphasis in action and characterization. The use of a revolving stage, which permitted the possibility of a degree of scenic background and yet left the forestage free for the actor to work with the spectator, was Reinhardt's modern compromise between illusion and non-illusion. At the Deutsches Theater the scene painter was replaced by the stage architect, and in the opinion of H. K. Moderwell among many others, Reinhardt's Shakespeare became "a model for the world."[3]

To trace Reinhardt's productions of Shakespeare over the ten-year span between *The Winter's Tale* of 1906 and the *Macbeth* of 1916 is to get a sense of his changing emphasis. The picture-book production of *The Winter's Tale* had, as we saw,[4] some of the simple, impressionistic features of symbolist design which made the play flow and work for a modern audience without really threatening Shakespeare's special qualities of psychological penetration, but in its colourful designs by Emil Orlik this production was basically a fantasy of illusion. So, too, was the *Romeo and Juliet* of 1907, decorated prettily by Karl Walser in the Victorian–Elizabethan manner. But the *Twelfth Night* of that year, performed in a boisterous vein of comedy to the music of Humperdinck, seemed to be a newly liberated creature. Its stage revolved with the curtain up, and the players prepared the spectator for the scene to come by a moment of brief pantomime as the scenic background changed, so that the audience was conscious of its own presence at the performance, helping to create the play – in the latest jargon, having a "metatheatrical" experience. This trickery was used again in 1912 for the musical treatment of *Much Ado about Nothing* as a light comedy, while the background glittered with crystal chandeliers and Venetian mirrors in a symbolist suggestion of Italian baroque.

The change was even more pronounced in the tragedies. For *King Lear* in 1908, designs by Karl Czeschka after the manner of Gordon Craig were taken to be starkly indicative of the feelings of conflict and cruelty which abound in the play, and the production seemed to anticipate expressionist drama in the intensity of its speech and the barbaric grimness of its setting. The *Hamlet* of 1909, with Moissi as the Prince, was thought by Kenneth Macgowan to be "an experience of life itself,"[5] but all that Reinhardt had done for the scenes on the battlements was to set off his actors by a cyclorama, against which shadowy figures moved almost in silhouette against a bleak and limitless North Sea of a cold and forbidding aspect; for the interior scenes all he had done was to provide a neutral curtain backing, with the mood of the scenes being changed by variations in costume, colour and lighting – the court in dark green, the Queen's chamber in red, and so on. Moissi made good use of the bare forestage, appearing to stand in the middle of the audience for the intimate psychological nuances of the soliloquies, an effect somewhat dissipated when the play was revived on the vast stage of the Grosses Schauspielhaus in 1920. This pattern was also followed for the *Othello* of 1910, with Albert Bassermann as the Moor on the forestage in full command of the house, the sets merely suggesting a street, a canal, a bridge or a harbour, so that the actors walked from one place to another as the stage turned, and the spirit of the tragedy was left to the power of Shakespeare's words in the mouth of the actor.

When Martin-Harvey brought Reinhardt's *The Taming of the Shrew* to the Prince of Wales Theatre, London, in 1909, the approach was quite without illusion: a forestage was built out over the footlights, and Christopher Sly and his make-believe wife were situated in the orchestra pit; the Players entered drawing a yellow and scarlet wagon and dressed in the style of the *commedia dell'arte*; and the Lord's servants changed the scene in full view of the audience. A traverse curtain of Italian baroque tapestry provided a decorative backing for the scene outside the alehouse, while the scenes on the main stage were dominated by white satin for the Lord's chamber and a background of blue and black for the sober banquet of the last act. Otherwise the only scenic setting as such was a terrace and balustrade upstage, accented with two round bay trees festooned with gold.

With the help of the promptbooks and contemporary reports, the rest of this chapter will look at three of Reinhardt's best-known Shakespeare productions: *A Midsummer Night's Dream*, *The Merchant of Venice* and *Macbeth*.

In January 1905, Reinhardt first presented what would become his favourite play, *A Midsummer Night's Dream*. It was this play which he continued to revive for thirty-four years, a span of time in which the production suffered many changes before it finally arrived in America. The actual itinerary was: Berlin (Neues Theater, 1905), Prague (1906), Berlin (Deutsches Theater, 1907), Budapest (1908), Munich (1909), Vienna and Munich again (1910), Berlin (Deutsches Theater again, 1913), Stockholm and Christiana (1915), six cities in Switzerland (1917), Berlin (Grosses Schauspielhaus, 1921), Vienna again (1925), Salzburg and New York (1927), Berlin (Deutsches Theater again, 1930), Florence and Oxford (1933), six cities in the United States (1934), Hollywood for the film (1935) and Hollywood on the stage (1939). Nobody has attempted to trace the production changes and the vagaries of performance over this long period, but the elements of baroque fantasy in the production were so much to Reinhardt's taste that it may be seen as his representative Shakespearian offering. He displayed his *A Midsummer Night's Dream* like a personal banner.

In its happy acceptance of imaginative licence, the production of 1905 was recognized as a new attack on the mood and style of the naturalistic movement, and the Austrian critic Rudolph Kommer named it the keystone of the director's career:

Reinhardt fought the royal battle against drab naturalism under the star of Shakespeare. It was not a German play that won the fight for romanticism of a new brand; it was the fanciful comedy, *A Midsummer Night's Dream*. Nothing could have suited Reinhardt's imaginative temperament better; no other play could have been more programmatic . . . It was a revelation. Berlin was jubilant. He had not added a word, he had not cut a line. And yet, it seemed a new play entirely. Full of life, colour, music and joy, it had a message that did away in one evening with all the voluptuous pessimism and sordidness of the preceding fifteen or twenty years of naturalism.[6]

With others by Shakespeare, this play had previously been treated in the ponderous style with which the German theatre approached the classics. Now it was freshly seen, the director's touch was quick and light, and the production brought together again all the arts of the theatre, including, in Felix Mendelssohn's score, the element of music that the naturalistic directors had inhibited.

The *Regiebuch* of 1905 is disappointing in that it gives little hint of how Reinhardt handled the variations in the lovers' quarrel, nowadays a test of a production's insights into the play's motifs and its mode of comedy, nor of how Puck (played in the early years by actresses – Gertrud Eysoldt or Leopoldine Konstantin) teased the lovers at the end of the scene, worked with the audience in the imaginary "darkness" of the wood, and magically arranged the sleeping bodies for the best results: we learn only that Lysander and Hermia are Right and that Demetrius and Helena are Left. But the *Regiebuch* is rich in those details by which Reinhardt indicated the stage setting and the appropriate business for the immortals. These details were unashamedly fantastic.

The early sets for the "wood near Athens" were lavishly impressionistic and ingeniously managed:

When the curtain goes up, the scene is covered with screens. Through these silver screens the moon shines palely, and slowly the light increases. The screens are raised slowly one after another in individual trails of mist. Streams trickle.

The scene is set with tall grass and many trees overhanging a clearing among them. At the back is a view of a high wooded hill which ends backstage. On the right is seen a lake glinting between the trees. On the left is the hillside. Past the lake on the left runs a fairly narrow path to the back of the stage.

The trees are very tall. The tops begin high up, so that the fairies appear very small. The tree-trunks must be as thick as possible. The roof of leaves is high up.

Moonlight, which falls in patches on the grass through the leaf pattern. The lake is lit from behind.[7]

Caverns and vistas could be discerned through the trees, and billows of smoke puffed from the ground. So it was that the first designer, Gustav Knina, was able to enhance the illusion of diminutive fairies and immense distances.

10   Shakespeare's *A Midsummer Night's Dream* at the Neues Theater, Berlin, in 1905, with Gertrud Eysoldt as Puck and Ellie Rothe as a fairy. Design by Gustav Knina and costume by Karl Walser.

This wood was central to the performance, as Heinz Herald recognized:

In the beginning was the wood. With the exception of the short overture of the opening scene and the big wedding finale, it is the setting for the whole play. It is its nurse, its native soil; from it everything flows, in it everyone is hidden, runs away, is mixed up, discovered, reconciled . . . It breathes, it is alive. It seems without beginning or end. It is inexhaustible, without visible limits, and yet, to sum up, it somehow represents every wood.[8]

Siegfried Jacobsohn also tried to account for the illusion of a supernatural world: "Moonlight shimmered, and dawn broke in a blaze of light. In the distance echoed earthly voices. Here and there a glowworm shone. Leaves rustled and twigs snapped."[9]

Macgowan reported that in the early years the wood was "a forest of real papier-maché trees,"[10] but when Ernst Stern was the designer in 1913, the heavy, three-dimensional trunks and rolling grass gave place to a more suggestive treatment of light and shade. Washburn-Freund considered it an almost symbolist effect of colour and light, creating an atmosphere of "endless woods, now threatening, now sheltering, full of mysterious sounds and beings."[11] Jacobsohn found everything very simple, but argued that "perhaps for that reason it was more evocative: when the spectator's imagination is receptive, then it is unnecessary to inflict a naturalistic production on him."[12] By the time the production had reached Vienna in 1925, the stage was virtually bare, a playing-space in front of green curtains which merely suggested the wood. The scenic display had become less obtrusive, and the stage was given over principally to the actors. When the production came to New York in 1927, Brooks Atkinson of the *New York Times* would not accept the verdict that it was merely "a pompous show." Reinhardt, he declared, "does not subordinate the play to showy effects; when he employs big set-pieces he does so merely to bring the play into its highest perspective."[13]

The *Regiebuch* indicates that great care was also given to the fairies. Here are some of the notes on their costumes:

A light, soft gauze covering their colours of lilac, violet, light and dark, then in all shades of green to dark green, and the same with a delicate light blue and dark blue. In the distance, an iridescent screen, rainbow-coloured, then shimmering with grey, white, gold and silver.

Also dresses like flowers, and, for example, like green grass with dewdrops (glass).

The children in flesh-coloured tights, and fitted with little quilted wings.

The wings various: white, multi-coloured, transparent and shining, big and little.

No shoes.[14]

Stern considered the immortals to be "a delight," although he did not approve of Eysoldt as Puck with "a piece of leopard skin round her bosom" – she was "a wraith of a girl instead of a broth of a boy." But he recognized that the fairies were "no longer the depressing ballerinas of old-fashioned performances, but slim and elegant girls in close-fitting green tights and green wigs."[15]

Everyone was impressed by the way Reinhardt made the wood come alive. Oberon was very much the central figure and the key to the play, and he first appeared apparently riding on a white stag with great antlers, and wearing a lighted crown upon his head. Then the *Regiebuch* suggests the activities of the fairy train:

His followers are trolls, dwarfs, gnomes and pixies, and they skip along behind and jump in front of him from the grass and the hill, down left, and tumble in his path.

Everything is alive. Everything is moving. Everyone skips, tumbles, jumps, runs and dances. A little later Titania hovers over the lake, and round her dance fairies with wings, others jump and skip in front of her. Mustardseed, Peaseblossom and Cobweb to the fore. Behind her six bigger fairies embrace in a circle.[16]

For Jacobsohn, the constant coming and going created "a total mobility which concealed how repetitive were the movements of individual fairies."[17] Herald found their movements entrancing: "gliding, jumping, hovering in a dance, flying over bush, stream and hillock." And he concluded, "Their motion is music, like their speech."[18]

On the line, "Ill met by moonlight / Proud Titania," the opposing kinds of fairy joined in combat, as the *Regiebuch* suggests: "The encounter is staged as a battle of flowers. Flowers fly to and fro, and the fairies menace one another with their wands, and romp and scuffle in the grass." When they come upon Lysander asleep beside Hermia, we read this:

A small fairy cautiously emerges from behind a tree, tiptoes gently at a distance round the sleepers with his bow, then dares to come closer, laughs and fetches a second fairy, with whom he runs forward swiftly, then back again laughing. Finally five come forward together, wind in a circle round the couple. They tickle the lovers on the nose and feet. The smallest sits astride Lysander.[19]

All this had the effect of making the lovers more ridiculous and an extension of the fantasy. And, needless to say, the unashamed sentimentality of these scenes made them immensely popular.

If Karl Walser's costumes for the lovers were conventionally Greek, the visual aspects of the production were otherwise telling. There were brilliant processionals under a star-spangled sky, with Theseus and Hippolyta making their entrance to a candle-lit parade, and much more. The invention of comic business for the mechanicals knew no bounds. The basic joke was their proclivity for falling down, but Quince was always hidden behind a voluminous script and Bottom was played as an amateur actor of all-consuming enthusiasm. Felix Felton, who later played Bottom in Reinhardt's Oxford University Dramatic Society production in 1933, records that throughout the play and even "on the night" a running argument raged between Bottom and Quince about the correct pronunciation of "Thisbe/Thisne." As each mechanical entered the wood, he was tripped up by Puck's arm "like a malevolent twig." Best of all, however, was Bottom's "Methought I had, methought I was" speech:

Usually this seems to go for very little. With Reinhardt, it began with a nervous groping, to see if the long snout and the long ears were still there; then a quickening of gesture, a nervous laughter; a sudden cut to silence; a fifty-yard run to the pond [a feature of the open-air set at Oxford]; a look at the reflection in the water; a scream of relief; and a jubilant dance off through the trees towards Athens.[20]

Felton added, "I don't know what impression this gives in print, but I can assure you that every night it held the audience like a vice."

The production at Oxford revealed some of Reinhardt's characteristics as a director. In New York, Brooks Atkinson had remarked that Reinhardt blessed the play with "limitless space"; the space at Oxford appeared to have blessed him. He had already enjoyed directing an open-air production in the grounds of his Schloss Leopoldskron at Salzburg in 1932, when he cast Isadora Duncan's students as fairies flitting in the twilight across the grass and devised a way of making Puck seem to materialize against the moonlight. At Oxford he had all the space he could have wanted, because he chose, not some convenient college garden, but the great meadow at South Park, Headington Hill, just beyond Magdalen Bridge, a great sloping field set with elm and beech and may, with a line of trees behind it through which a further meadow could be seen, and a wood and bushes on either side. An apocryphal story is told that when Reinhardt caught a glimpse of the village over the hill, he cried, "That town – it must go!"

The correspondent of *The Daily Telegraph* suggested that, once out in the open, Reinhardt thought in terms "not of square feet but of acres."[21] The production became an unique exercise in the use of space and light, with all the emphasis on the immortals (some eighty supers), and a certain athleticism demanded of the players. *The Times* approved:

In such a theatre there is nothing the fairies may not do. Puck may mock his victims from branches above their heads or from the swift invisibility offered him by a hole in the ground; Oberon's troop and Titania's, advancing from opposite woods, may meet by sudden chance and vanish, when their encounter is over, like the legions of a dream.

But the writer saw that the play's focus was somewhat altered:

No longer is it a story of mortals in this world behind whom an enchantment has arisen; it is a tale of sprites and goblins pursuing the natural life of their own dwelling place, into which men and women have blindly wandered. That it has been Professor Reinhardt's purpose to enforce this emphasis to create an illusion of immortal intimacy becomes increasingly clear as the evening passes.

Some loss of individual character and neglect of the text were also inevitable: the image of Titania, played by the Swedish dancer Nini Theilade, lay "in her movement and appearance rather than in the music of her words."[22]

It was a little embarrassing to watch the actors traversing such great distances and making breathless entrances and exits at the double. Rupert Hart-Davis in the *Spectator* thought this dispelled some of the magic:

The ladies seldom had more than 100 yards sprint to negotiate – no inconsiderable feat in their elaborate dresses – but the men covered all distances up to and including the half-mile. One competitor suddenly dashed along the footlights and, much to the delight of the audience, failed to clear the water-jump [the pond mentioned above]. Often during an intimate scene in the foreground one's eye was caught by some lonely player plodding wearily round the furthest fringe of the meadow, the last lap of the three-miles cross-country.[23]

The Daily Telegraph praised Puck for running far and fast enough to establish a good claim to a cross-country Blue, "if he has not got one already." So the wits had their field-day, but no one denied that the effects produced were justified.

The play had never been "more lovely to the eye, nor has it ever partaken more fully of the nature of a dream" (*The Times*). Concealed lights under the trees and in the grass made it possible for fairies to appear and disappear: "Points of light danced and twinkled through the trees, the music grew seemingly odd and unearthly; we were back in the Golden Age." Titania made a dancing entrance from afar across the meadow, leading a small child dressed in white, so that even Hart-Davis was enchanted: "Her long deep-blue train held shoulder-high by following sprites, her dance between the trees and subsequent disappearance into the darkness on the shoulder of a satyr will not easily be forgotten" (*Spectator*). The mechanicals approached their rendezvous in the wood by several separate paths across the meadow, their lanterns converging in the darkness. Puck's ability to vanish abruptly by dropping into a pit made the audience gasp. And when he carried off a fairy into the night, Felton described how "a slowly narrowing spotlight followed the undulations of her hands to a pin-point of light in the darkness."[24]

Had the play been sacrificed to the producer? *The Times* felt not. On the contrary, "it has been freshly seen, freshly interpreted, and performed in accordance with its woodland circumstance and an artist's dominating idea . . . At its peaks it is a production to take the breath away."

The Shakespeare play in Reinhardt's repertory which had a comparable impact in Europe deserves a mention here. It was *The Merchant of Venice*, first produced at the Deutsches Theater in November 1905, the year of the momentous *Dream*. Its itinerary was not quite so extensive. Between 1905 and 1935 it visited Prague, Budapest, Vienna, Munich, Bucharest, Copenhagen and Stockholm, with four return visits to Berlin before being presented over a canal in Venice itself. The first Shylock was Rudolf Schildkraut (replaced by Albert Bassermann in 1913 and Moissi in 1918); Portia was played by Agnes Sorma (later by Else Heims, but in Venice by Pirandello's Marta Abba) and Reinhardt himself was Tubal.

Again the play's "environment," rather than its actual setting, became the object of the director's efforts. In Emil Orlik's original design in 1905, the streets of Venice were built on a revolve, but the traditional gondolas and merry-makers were discarded for a true Venetian world that came alive on the stage. The life of the city was subtly backed by the sound of singing and distant violins, as well as by Humperdinck's joyful music, which Bruno Walter, then conductor at the Vienna Opera, recalled as being blended ominously with an almost imperceptible march.[25] It was a Renaissance world, or so the Danish critic Georg Brandes reported:

The scenes of Italian life not only made you realize the quick pulse of that people, but also the impetuous festive spirit of the early Renaissance. The stage pictures were reminders of paintings by Carpaccio, then by Giovanni Bellini, again by Paris Bordone or Paolo Veronese. The headdresses and costumes, the carriage and gestures of the actors were of the year 1500.[26]

It was also a Latin world, thought Jacobsohn:

The Venetian joy of living is the dominant note of the performance; Jewish suffering is only a dissonant note. Everyone erupts and jumps for joy . . . and Shakespeare's love poetry, which comes alive by moonlight and love-song and is as fragrant as a dream, is captured in the Deutsches Theater in a nocturne which is incomparable in its delightful tenderness.[27]

Dieter Hoffmeier went so far as to say that "the hero, the centre, the heart and essence of the performance was – Venice. Not Shylock, but Venice. That ever-singing, ever-buzzing Venice. A city which rejoiced in the joy of life, its pleasure, delight and exuberance. Which felt like the capital and centre of the world."[28]

Shylock may not have been at the centre of the production, but for the first time in his work with Shakespeare Reinhardt felt the challenge of a major, complicated figure, and the *Regiebuch* speaks for his new quality of care and detail in delineating his character's every gesture and move. Nowhere was this more apparent than in the scene

11   Shakespeare's *The Merchant of Venice* at the Deutsches Theater, Berlin, in 1905. Design by Emil Orlik.

of the trial, which in the view of Macgowan and Jones was built up to a pitch of "intolerable excitement."[29] Shylock was exactly observed. He entered the court "with a slow step, as perfectly in control of himself as at the beginning of the play, richly dressed and almost stonelike in his hate, armed with a sinister calm." Like a stone he listened to the Duke, "without moving, giving nothing away."

The shape of the feeling in the scene was partly determined by the director's exact control of the crowd, and he did not hesitate to write individual lines for it after the manner of the Meiningen company. Thus, when Shylock raised his voice on

> by our holy Sabbath have I sworn
> To have the due and forfeit of my bond,

there was a great commotion throughout the court, and the following lines by Reinhardt were spoken together:

DUKE (*strongly*). No, Shylock, no! you may not have that.
BASSANIO (*emptying a bag of coins on the table, left*). Here is the money, you Jew; take three times the sum.
GRATIANO. Unfeeling Jew, shame! We won't stand for this.
SALARINO. On your life, let justice be done!
SOLANIO. A wolf rules your doglike spirit.
FIRST JUDGE. Not even the metal of the executioner's axe has half the edge of your bitter resentment.
SECOND JUDGE. Shylock, listen to us!
THIRD JUDGE. Let charity be your guide, Shylock!

Shylock let this uproar subside to silence, and then spoke calmly.

The rhythm of the scene was precisely timed, and each exchange precisely heard, like this between Shylock and Portia:

PORTIA. Shylock, there's thrice thy money offered thee.
SHYLOCK. An oath, an oath, I have an oath in heaven.
Shall I lay perjury upon my soul?
No, not for Venice.

Reinhardt here added the direction for Portia's line, "*quietly, shaking her head*," and for Shylock's lines, "*plainly, unemotionally, clipped*," so that all feeling was restrained until the last, although beneath the surface it was running tempestuously. Shylock remained outwardly controlled, while "trembling with inner excitement," and everyone "stared at him speechlessly." Not until Portia sprang her surprise on,

> Tarry a little, there is something else.
> This bond doth give thee here no jot of blood,

did the whole stage erupt. At this crisis, Reinhardt wrote, "Everyone turns suddenly and stares at Portia. Bassanio slowly rises. The judges rise. Then suddenly a cry of relief rings out, as with one voice, [followed by] laughter."[30]

Reinhardt came to *Macbeth* at a comparatively late date: 1916. It had not been one of the plays of the 1913 Shakespeare Festival, perhaps because *Hamlet, King Lear* and *Othello* had taxed the company enough on that occasion. When Reinhardt at last directed *Macbeth*, he gave unusually close attention to the psychological motivation of his principals, as the *Regiebuch* amply suggests. The production at the Deutsches Theater was, of course, interesting for other things: Ernst Stern's setting of rocks and battlements darkly silhouetted against the cyclorama; the striking use of an organ during the scene of Duncan's murder to provide a deep rumbling offstage, against which were heard the piercing notes of the screech-owl; and the Witches with angular shapes like agile skeletons dancing in a green light in a frenzied orgy, with a giantess for Hecate towering over them and a touch of cannibalism when they fought over the "finger of birth-strangled babe" as it was tossed into the pot. But the production was outstanding for the detail with which Reinhardt worked out every tone and gesture for Macbeth and his Lady, as played by Paul Wegener and Hermione Körner (later by Emil Jannings and Elisabeth Bergner).

Marvin Rosenberg has assessed Wegener's deepening perception of his role as he performed it over a period of years:

Wegener had begun as a barbarian Macbeth, brutal, nearly animal, playing in a naturalistic, Hauptmann-influenced style; his next Macbeth was more of a gentleman, as a king elegant and royal, but troubled by a conscience he could only stifle by new atrocities. Going deeper for Reinhardt, who saw Macbeth as a neurotic, Wegener's strong warrior's mask covered a deep, relentless anxiety: at times he seemed almost a somnabulist, at others a son of chaos, yielding in anxiety to physical weakness, consumed by the kind of insatiable turbulence that recalled Matkowsky [Adalbert Matkowsky, who had played the part in Berlin in 1901 like a nervous wreck]. Lady Macbeth, in this equation, was worn away and destroyed by the very force of his *angst.*[31]

It was this more sensitive Macbeth who can be perceived through Reinhardt's annotations in every key scene in the play.

When Macbeth first met the Witches, he was already somewhat obsessed, and Reinhardt had him speak the line, "So foul and fair a day I have not seen," in the same rhythm the audience had heard from the Witches themselves in the first scene. He stared at them speechlessly, and, gasping for air, spoke in a low, clipped voice. On the third hail, "All hail, Macbeth, that shalt be King hereafter!" he

12 Shakespeare's *Macbeth* at the Deutsches Theater, Berlin, in 1916.
The Witches.

trembled and seemed to change colour, and when Banquo questioned him, he dropped his eyes and could not move. On Macbeth's words, "Stay, you imperfect speakers!" they stood motionless and stared at him, compelling him to speak his next lines to them almost apologetically. After they vanished, he was left in a state of nervous exhaustion, breathing hard, wiping the sweat from his face and neck, running trembling fingers over his face. When Ross entered and greeted him as Cawdor with "Hail, most worthy thane!" ominously echoing the Witches' words, it made Macbeth lift his hand to his forehead as if to ward off a blow. The same gesture enabled him to hide the expression on his face, and he paid his courtesies to Ross and Angus without looking at them, merely gesturing to the air. He waited until the others were out of earshot, deliberately moving away from them to conceal his feelings before he hissed to himself, "I am Thane of Cawdor." Then he swallowed, gasping for air and raising his hands to his chest before they dropped to his sides again, drained of life. When in the next scene Macbeth greeted the King, he could not look him in the eyes.

Reinhardt's Lady Macbeth was highly emotional and quickly excited. She read the letter very slowly at first, pausing a little before the mention of Cawdor, but on "Hail King that shalt be!" she let drop the hand holding the letter, and stared ahead of her for a long pause. When she finished reading, she repeated the gesture of letting her hand drop. After another look at the letter, she began to pace up and down, slowly at first, then more and more quickly, suggesting her growing excitement and resolution. In her subsequent soliloquy, she took a deep breath before the line, "Yet do I fear thy nature," speaking more slowly and with a kind smile, as if she had had problems with her husband before: there was affection and concern for him, with a pause before "Hie thee hither!" that indicated an intense longing for his return. Thus, when the two at last came together, she spoke to him tenderly, even sensually, but never forgetting her chief object. Her "Oh, never / Shall sun that morrow see" was spoken with fierce energy, but immediately afterwards she looked him in the eyes tenderly, and stroked his brow slowly and lovingly. She hissed "Be the serpent!" and by the end of her speech her breast, neck and nostrils swelled, she breathed deeply, her eyes sparkled, she grasped him by the hand and spoke in a joyful undertone. Nevertheless, in the presence of Duncan later in the act, her face was again a mask.

The stresses and strains of the scenes of Duncan's murder were finely calculated. Macbeth gloried neurotically in his "dagger of the mind," and finally hid the real thing instinctively behind his back, and listened and stood deathly still as the lights upstage were extinguished. He lowered his voice and took two soft steps to centrestage on "thus with his stealthy pace, / With Tarquin's ravishing strides," moving to the rhythm of the verse. He approached Duncan's chamber up the stairs of the set, still listening, and at the ringing of the bell giving a start and coming to an abrupt halt, wiping sweat from his forehead with the hand that held the dagger.

On Lady Macbeth's cautious entrance, she looked about her, speaking with bated breath, stopping suddenly to listen, until she herself began to creep up the stairs, craning her neck. Then she put her ear to the ground and retreated down in fear to hide herself. Only when she perceived her husband did she emerge again, her hand over her mouth, speaking with strong emotion and tense pauses before running to him across the stage.

Macbeth met her with staring eyes, his voice hoarse and his face contorted with horror on "One cried Murther," while his Lady moaned and shook her head in alarm and looked about her. They were positioned close together on the empty stage downstage left. At the suggestion that he must return to the scene to smear the grooms with blood, she pushed him a step or two until he resisted and warded her off with a shudder. She tried to take the daggers from him as he stood in a daze; then she ordered, "Give me the daggers!" Finally, she had to pry them from his clenched fingers.

Her own exit was quick. Hiding the daggers in her clothing, she looked about her hastily and was up the stairs in a flash, her silhouette and shadow seen hurrying along high up against the window. Macbeth was left alone in his trance, paralysed, unable to flee, staring at the blood on his hands and turning them over again and again. When Lady Macbeth returned, she was already rubbing blood from her hands in her horror, anticipating the sleep-walking scene, but controlling herself with a superhuman effort, even assuming a brighter voice and attempting to smile.

In the scenes that followed, Lady Macbeth increasingly broke down from sleeplessness, although, as the text requires, Macbeth at first gained in self-assurance. The changes in him were clearly marked by Reinhardt's touches: a deep breath exhaled through the lips after he had given his intructions to the murderers of Banquo; he laughed and clapped his hands with the Lords in the banquet scene. But it was in this scene that he broke down again. When he saw the Murderer who had come to report Banquo's death, Macbeth filled himself a bowl of wine and wandered across to where he stood, hissing the line, "There's blood upon thy face," over his shoulder as he pretended to drink. When he heard of Fleance's escape, he set the bowl on the table and stared before him trembling, as if in something of his former trance. At the end of the exchange, he stood darkly brooding until all eyes turned on him, the table fell quiet and Macbeth himself heard the silence.

Reinhardt made the most of the recurring visual motif of blood in this and other scenes. Banquo's ghost, when he appeared, had dreadful, bulging eyes, with his forehead bleeding from a great wound that was shaped like a crucifix. Lady Macbeth first spoke in a loud voice, "Sit, worthy friends!" and then, smiling faintly as if unconcerned, moved among the guests, trying to reassure them in a lower voice. At length, concealing her face and gnashing her teeth, she turned on Macbeth harshly with "Are you a man?" until she saw his stricken look and brought her hands together in shocked surprise, the sound drawing all eyes upon them again. Macbeth's reaction to the first appearance of the Ghost was horrifying: he repeatedly passed one hand over his face as if to wipe the vision from his eyes, while he stared at the red wine that had spilled over his other hand like blood. He recovered somewhat before the Ghost's second entrance, able to toast "our dear friend Banquo" with cheerful bravado and with only a little hesitation on the name, but on "Avaunt and quit my sight!" he threw the bowl to the ground, his whole body shaking. Thereafter he returned to his former trancelike state, brooding on "Can such things be, / And overcome us like a summer's cloud . . .?" like a shattered man, but ending the scene with a savage smile on his face for "I am in blood / Stepp'd in so far . . ."[32]

Much of this gesturing will today seem excessive; it was done, of course, in the inflated, classical acting-style of its time. But in the consistency of character portrayal, the reiteration of touches of character and behaviour, the awareness of a repeating word or phrase, of a recurring motif in the action, in the perception of a rhythm and shape in the whole play, Reinhardt proved himself to be equal to the demands of Shakespearian tragedy.

6   A style for every play

The plays of the German, Italian, French and Greek classical theatres were of such unfamiliar and unreal conventions that it was important that a production hit precisely the mode of performance which would carry a modern audience. Having made it a point of principle to accept the challenge of almost every great drama of the past, Reinhardt experimented to recapture its spirit and style in a way that was never merely antiquarian, but showed the expanding theatre of the West how it could know its own heritage at first hand.

Reinhardt was unequalled in his devotion to the classics of the German theatre, particularly the plays of Lessing, Goethe and Schiller, but also others by Kotzebue, Kleist and Hebbel. In particular, Reinhardt's work with Goethe's *Faust* spanned a lifetime in the theatre, beginning with Part I at the Deutsches Theater in 1909, continuing with eighty-five performances of Part II in 1911, and experimenting in 1920 with the barer outlines of the *Urfaust* sketches which had come to light in 1887. He finally returned to Part I for the Salzburg Festival of 1933, reviving this production every year until 1937, and then shipping it to the California Festival of 1938 in Hollywood and San Francisco. Writing in 1924, E. J. Dent observed,

It is rightly inevitable that all the methods of the German theatre should be centred on *Faust*; that all technical devices of staging, acting, music or anything else, should be regarded as means to its performance; and that this play of all plays should set the example to playwrights, producers and everyone connected with the theatre.[1]

It follows that Reinhardt's now legendary performances of *Faust*, encrusted with the comments and notes of some thirty years, deserved book-length treatment in themselves, and they did, indeed, achieve this in 1968 in a Munich dissertation by Wilfried Passow, a study which reproduces the *Regiebuch* for Part I and adds an extended commentary. Here we shall touch on only two or three of the characteristics of Reinhardt's production over the years, those chiefly reflecting its scenic and atmospheric quality.

In all the productions, required changes of twenty or more scenes presented a major challenge, but also the major opportunity to capture the quality and mood of the original. For the productions of Parts I and II in 1909 and 1911, Alfred Roller designed the scenes and Ernst

13   Goethe's *Faust* at the Deutsches Theater, Berlin, in 1909, with Lucie
Höflich as Gretchen and Friedrich Kayssler as Faust; design by Alfred
Roller.

Stern the costumes after Dürer, and the use of a revolve went a long
way towards solving the problem. The proportions of Part II were
particularly epic, having a cast of 108 and a playing time of seven
hours, excluding an hour for dinner. For a play in which Goethe
parades on stage a sheer pageant, a series of tableaux of historical
and allegorical figures to represent the tide of human progress,
ingenuity was above all the order of the day: on Walpurgis Night,
Faust, Mephistopheles and Homunculus wander endlessly to the
music of Schumann over the Plains of Pharsalus, and only a bare
stage or a convenient revolve could have served. Nevertheless, each
scene was a gem: the finale of the heavenly hosts was as if "painted
by Fra Angelico on a gold background, a mosaic of angelic lines filling the space, faint, without shadows, like disembodied spirits, whilst
only a slightly heightened glow of light surrounds the Blessed Virgin
in a dreamlike aureole."[2] With many scenes crammed on the revolve,
it necessarily meant that they were small in scale, but this limitation

of scenic space also helped to focus the subjects of the play – the narrow medieval streets, Faust's confined study, the witches' kitchen, Auerbach's wine cellar, Gretchen's tiny room.

For the *Urfaust* of 1920, another device was tried. Inside the proscenium arch of the Deutsches Theater was built a tall Gothic arch of only nine foot width. This was to be the permanent set, although the upper traceries of the arch, flown from above, were able to vary the height of the "window." In this way each scene could be a set-piece, a tableau totally framed and focused, each decorated like a medieval woodcut. Thus the scene of Faust (Paul Hartmann) in his study showed the scholar cramped at his desk, with Mephistopheles (Ernst Deutsch) approaching him from one side as the heavenly spirits

14 Goethe's *Faust* at the Felsenreitschule, Salzburg, in 1933, with design by Clemens Holzmeister and costume by Herbert Ploberger. The witches' kitchen.

watched from on high. The narrow arch could also readily suggest the narrow streets of Wittenberg, and the traceries were raised for the scene in the cathedral square, showing women kneeling by a pillar on the steps of the church, their backs to the audience. The ceiling was lowered again for Auerbach's cellar, realistically suggesting an environment suitable for four men drinking in a tavern. The lovelorn Gretchen (Helene Thimig) was posed like a madonna in her little room, a patch of golden sky seen through the window, or confined under a low vault in the prison scene. The effect of all this was so solemn and beautiful that Dent wondered whether the play was being performed for the pictures it created, rather than that the pictures were being created for the play.

A further experiment with staging *Faust* followed Reinhardt's decision to present the play in the open air of the summer riding school (the Felsenreitschule) of the Prince Archbishop at the Salzburg Festival in 1933. With Clemens Holzmeister as his designer, nothing less than a *"Fauststadt,"* a Faust town, was built, and grew from year to year:

There were trees, bushes and flowers which had been planted in the first year of the production and then grew from summer to summer: in Marthe's garden, near Gretchen's house, under the Lindentree close to the gate of the town, moon and stars joined in the play and gusts of the night wind led from a sultry evening to the pallid dawn of the dungeon scene.[3]

With his customary thoroughness, Reinhardt took notes every night, and the production grew too.

The Salzburg *Regiebuch* notes, though characteristically practical, strongly convey the atmosphere of the production. Reinhardt was above all things concerned to create the correct mood. The heavenly hosts stood on top of a high rock, with a medieval town on the stage below. The town was made up of a cluster of poor houses squeezed together. Cathedral steps led off to the right, and in the middle stood a town gate, through which a dark alley could be seen. As the play began, sounds told the story and painted the scene:

Evening is drawing on. The town is falling asleep. There is light in the windows. A bell tolls. Servant girls at the fountain. Songs. Night-watchmen. Barking dogs. Human voices sing. A horn. Students stagger home bawling from a tavern. A woman's voice. A window, a door shuts. A bolt and chain. The lights gradually go out.

Only Faust's light did not go out, and he was still seen through his window sitting at his lamp. As darkness descended on the town below, it grew bright high above the houses for "the prologue in heaven," and, as the music swelled, a magic light transformed the mountainside into an unreal vision, with silver trees on silver clouds (Reinhardt's notes at this point suggest that he was worried about his angels standing on a bridge of clouds with no protective railing). The moonlight turned pale and Faust's lamp burned low, a ghostly red light falling on his face.

Faust's study was crammed with the tools of the alchemist, his heavy table full of papers and books, a reading desk, phials and retorts. On the wall, shelves with more papers, glasses and flasks. An alchemist's fire and chimney, with many receptacles. The witches' kitchen was a hole in the rock, a cave in half-darkness, illuminated by a low, flickering fire, its smoke rising round a bubbling cauldron. All around were the instruments of witchcraft: a glass ball, mirrors and glasses, the heads of animals and skeletons, crucibles and flasks, plants and roots, broomsticks. Stalactites hung from the ceiling. There was an armchair made from crooked branches. Long-tailed monkeys swung from the walls. Owls hooted. Cats howled. Doll-like figures twisted in the coloured light and seemed to dance up and down. And for the *Walpurgisnacht* the set consisted of a mountain path lit by

15   The *"Fauststadt"* for Goethe's *Faust* at the Felsenreitschule, Salzburg, in 1933. Design model by Clemens Holzmeister.

moonlight, with barren trees and the wind sighing through their crooked boughs, slamming doors and windows, whistling down the chimneys, bending the trees until they groaned. The *Regiebuch* also includes a reminder to prepare *"Dampfapparate!"* – vapour equipment.[4]

Yet, Granville-Barker reported that the acting-style was direct, real and vital:

How many a Margaret have we seen strolling down some medieval Bond-street, to be accosted by a proper young gentleman with the polite offer of his arm, to whom she will reply with unruffled sweetness that she is not a lady nor a beauty, all the while as conscious as we are that if she were not undisguisably both she would not have been engaged for the part. At the Deutsches Theater a quite unromantic-looking girl is hurrying home from church. She is stopped abruptly, spoken to almost fiercely by this gaunt Faust. She is as terrified as a girl would be, stares at him with wide-opened eyes, gasps out a sentence or two, shakes him off with no pretence at politeness and runs home as hard as she can.[5]

Reinhardt forgot nothing, and Adler considered that "the indescribable effect of the *Fauststadt* was the indisputable proof of the necessity of his requests. Nothing was left to chance: no step, no sound, no ray of light, nor even darkness. Everything blended like the movement of the stars in the firmament."[6] Unfortunately, however, Reinhardt failed to reckon with the unpredictable Salzburg weather, and the first night of *Faust* in 1933 was visited by a cloudburst just before the play was to have begun. In the years that followed, Reinhardt erected a cover over the spectators without completely eliminating the effects of night that he wanted.

The spontaneity of an Italian *commedia dell'arte* performance, with its acrobatic tumbling and capering, its near-balletic pantomime and a killing pace, makes an obvious appeal to a director with a flair. Not that Reinhardt was free to recreate the improvisatory element that made the original *commedia* a thing of exciting interaction between stage and audience, encouraging the unpredictable growth of the play in performance. Reinhardt's *commedia* style was strictly controlled, line by line, gesture by gesture, like everything else he attempted. It might be better compared with the more refined, more sophisticated *commedia* style of the eighteenth century. Indeed, Carlo Gozzi's fairy-tale of *Turandot* (1762), done not in the Schiller version, but by Karl Vollmoeller, who would next supply the scenario for *The Miracle*, in 1911 provided Reinhardt with a first vehicle for this extravagant kind of comedy, and prompted a special issue of the Deutsches Theater Papers, the *Blätter des Deutschen Theaters*.

Gozzi's story of the cruel Chinese princess Turandot and the handsome prince Calaf, who must answer her three riddles or forfeit his life, unexpectedly included such comic court officers as Pantalone for the major-domo, Tartaglia for the lord high chancellor, Brighella as captain of the imperial pages and even Truffaldino as chief eunuch in charge of the harem. The production was rich with the evocative music of Ferruccio Busoni and Johann Wijman, and lavish with Stern's "porcelain fantasy" of Chinese rococo settings: Turandot's harem was hung with coloured lights in purple, red and blue, and Calaf's room was a rhapsody in purple, lit by orange lamps over a purple and green bed against a purple background. As Huntly Carter reported them, the Chinese costumes were "quaint, gorgeous, and splendid . . . moving riotously in rich masses," and he was especially delighted by "dazzling processions of soldiers, slaves, lampbearers, composing themselves against the curtains of the two-coloured butterflies and dragons."[7] Everything was free fantasy, gloriously unreal.

Although a whole book has been devoted to Reinhardt's work on the *commedia dell'arte*,[8] he found few opportunities to explore the genre further. He had produced Goldoni's *The Servant of Two Masters* (1743) at the Kammerspiele in 1907, but it was not until 1924 that he tackled the style again with the help of the great family of actors, the Thimigs: Hugo playing Pantalone, Hermann as Truffaldino and Helene as Smeraldina. This production, embroidered with the music of Mozart like a comic opera, and brilliantly dressed by Oskar Laske and Karl Witzmann in the costume of a harlequinade, began its career in Vienna at the Theater in der Josefstadt, moved later that year to the Komödie in Berlin, and thereafter travelled everywhere, finally becoming part of the San Francisco and Hollywood Workshops in 1939–40. When it was presented at the Cosmopolitan Theatre in New York in 1928, the *New York Times* was delighted with the "fearless fantasticality" of its characterizations and the "shameless abandon" of its clowning. Before this visit, the play had been virtually unknown in America, and the *commedia* something of a mystery.

It was nevertheless the drama of Molière that best displayed Reinhardt's idea of the high style of classical comedy, and in this he made good use of two great comedians, first Viktor Arnold and then Max Pallenberg. In his occasional addresses to the actors, Reinhardt had from the start linked the names of Shakespeare and Molière as the standard for achievement in acting. Beginning with *George Dandin* in 1912, with Arnold in the title part, he established a kind of "Molière stage" at the Deutsches Theater, even before that of Jacques Copeau at the Vieux Colombier. It consisted of a platform set against a permanent, formal, symmetrical garden pavilion, in order that the movements and gestures of the actors should be seen in silhouette or relief. On this stage he also displayed his musicians in the appropriate period costume, always supporting with music the action of the main characters as well as the moves of the servants between the acts. The total effect was one of exquisite comic distancing, of a performance in which style itself contributed not only to the audience's aesthetic pleasure, but also to its perception of the comedy.

The success of *The Imaginary Invalid* in 1916 turned on the performance of Pallenberg as Argan, a vision of hypochondria wrapped in a dressing-gown and buried among the pillows piled high upon the armchair in his sickroom, with an arsenal of bottles and phials, glasses and bowls, to the right and left of him. There he lay, swallowing his medicines, gulping down his powders, doubling up with imagined aches and pains. The production offered a nice balance between scenes presented with only the bare necessities of stage decoration, and three ballets of Moorish girls and gipsies done in magnificent style to force the contrast with life in Argan's house. However, the extraordinary achievement here on Reinhardt's part was to have offered the Berlin public a French play as an antidote to the war with France.

Criticism of *The Miser* of 1917, done in a controversial version by Carl Sternheim the comic expressionist, ranged from outright condemnation to enthusiastic approval. Reinhardt had again cast Pallenberg in the central part, this time presenting him as a dwarf-like figure dressed in shabby clothing, with a green face peering through dull, gummy eyes and falling tufts of hair. The dialogue was as spare as Harpagon's room, but Reinhardt introduced a modern sympathy, a new subtlety and even emotion into the scene with the spendthrift son Cléante (played by the young Hermann Thimig). When Cléante left his father in act I, the miser's voice failed him: "He wiped tears from his eyes, his nose watered, he pressed his purse to his heart, and groaning and sighing laid his forehead on the lattice-window and stared out: a close of complete silence."[9]

Some of the controversy surrounded Sternheim's expressionistic "ballet-pantomimes." The third act, set in Harpagon's garden, included a dream of Cléante's in which Harpagon wooed a pretty young girl; when she in turn was attracted by a handsome young man, a shower of gold pieces distracted the old man from his purpose as a lover. An earlier pantomime in act II had been cut by the censor for its erotic suggestiveness: Sternheim had called for a pretty

16   Goldoni's *The Servant of Two Masters* at the Theater in der
Josefstadt, Vienna, in 1924, with Helene Thimig as Smeraldina and
Hermann Thimig as Truffaldino.

girl to emerge from a bed recess and give Cléante a low curtsy. However, other moments were totally successful. Reinhardt expanded Molière's final line, in which Harpagon announces that he is off to see *"ma chère cassette,"* so that it became an extension of the scene: alone on the stage at the end, Pallenberg took a deep breath, slid along the wall and shut all the doors, clutching his darling cash-box all the time, chuckling faintly, murmuring tenderly to his treasure, covering his gold with kisses.

Apart from a brief encounter with Euripides' *Medea* in 1904, Reinhardt came late to the Greeks. When he did turn to them in 1910 and 1911 in a famous season at the Circus Schumann in Berlin, he succeeded, according to Pilikian, in initiating "the first large-scale revival of the classical Greek drama in over 2,000 years."[10] Large-scale indeed: the Circus Schumann was about the size of the Albert Hall in London.

Reinhardt's *Lysistrata* had charmed everyone with its gaiety in 1908. This had been accomplished by a singing, dancing, celebrating crowd in the last part of the play, a "high-water mark of Reinhardt's stagecraft." At the end, the cast

manifests the many and varied emotions of the inhabitants of the delivered city, which has been handed back to Eros. Colours race all over the scene, lines (formed of dancers) advance and recede, entwine, break, and joyously melt away. There are shouts of laughter, singing, and every expression of pent-up emotion. In the background, at a distance, are seen the lights of the condemned town; from afar come cries and murmurs, mixed with laughter and shouting, which gradually increase until they merge with the others in one mighty climax of joy, and the curtain falls on one of the finest pantomimic climaxes provided by Reinhardt.[11]

So much for Greek comedy. When Reinhardt touched the tragic choruses of Sophocles and Aeschylus, his talent for mass effects found a new and more powerful direction.

The production of *Lysistrata* had started life very modestly at the Kammerspiele in Berlin, and proved itself in travelling to Budapest, Breslau, Frankfurt, Vienna and Munich over a period of two years; after the war, it was finally revived at the Grosses Schauspielhaus in 1920. Sophocles' *Oedipus Rex* in Hofmannsthal's translation, and designed by Alfred Roller with costumes by Stern, travelled endlessly. Beginning in the Festhalle in Munich in 1910, it went to Vienna and Budapest before it was performed in the Circus Schumann in Berlin itself. Next year it was on its way to Riga, St Petersburg, Stock-

17 Sophocles' *Oedipus Rex* at the Circus Schumann, Berlin, in 1910,
with design by Alfred Roller and costume by Ernst Stern.

holm, Prague, Budapest again, Zurich, Berlin again, Amsterdam and The Hague before it received its celebrated production in English at Covent Garden, London, in January 1912, while the German company continued on again to St Petersburg, Moscow, Riga, Warsaw, Kiev, Odessa and Stockholm. This play was revived in 1916 and 1917 at the Berlin Volksbühne, although it unaccountably never achieved the Grosses Schauspielhaus. Over the years, Wegener and Moissi played Oedipus, and Rosa Bertens and Tilla Durieux played Jocasta; Reinhardt himself even played Teiresias in 1911.

The *Oresteia* of Aeschylus in Vollmoeller's translation was also produced in Munich in 1911, before proceeding to the Circus Schumann. It was designed by Roller, with Moissi as Orestes. Apart from being in the repertory for a six-month tour of Switzerland in 1917, and reaching the Grosses Schauspielhaus in 1919, this production did not have the same varied life enjoyed by *Oedipus Rex*. We may therefore turn to the latter in order to sample Reinhardt's sense of the Greek occasion.

In Munich's Musikfesthalle in 1910, Reinhardt had found a large hall to match his vast conception of the play, and for the first time he directed without the disguises and spatial restrictions of a proscenium arch. The acting area was a large semicircle, round which were set backing screens in black with the suggestion of a central entrance. Sir John Martin-Harvey had seen this treatment in the Circus Schumann, and was "simply overwhelmed." Thereafter Reinhardt looked always for an arena theatre, some sort of "circus" for this play, and as early as July 1911 began the search in London for a large old-fashioned theatre with its galleries set far enough back for the floor to be used as a Greek *orchestra*. The Albert Hall itself was considered, but Martin-Harvey reported with regret that although "prize-fights and operettas" were welcome there, "the greatest tragedy of ancient Greece was banned by the terms of the Hall's charter."[12] The production was eventually mounted in the huge Theatre Royal, Covent Garden, where it played for three weeks before it went on tour. The translation was by Gilbert Murray, whose translations of Euripides had been well received; some adjustments were made by W. L. Courtney. Martin-Harvey played Oedipus in a much-praised performance, Lillah McCarthy played Jocasta as a compassionate wife and mother, and Louis Calvert was a shrewd and cautious Creon. But their work had little to do with yet another "overwhelming" treatment.

For a setting, the whole proscenium opening at Covent Garden was filled with the former black screens arranged to represent the façade of the palace. To these were now added a pair of massive doors of burnished copper, which, according to the *Morning Post*, were "splashed with the blood-red of a sun setting angrily in the west."[13] Heavy black pillars stood on either side, and a great flight of steps, as wide as the proscenium arch itself, led down to the *orchestra*. There were three platforms or landings on the steps, one on each side for altars and one in the centre for the principals. The orchestra pit was covered over, together with three or four rows of stalls, to accommodate a projecting altar, and the raked floor of the house was raised so that Oedipus should not have to stand below the level of the spectators. A wide gangway was constructed to run from the back of the stalls to the new stage, and the whole arrangement was lit from the front by lights placed at the back of the stalls. From the moment at the beginning when these lights were slowly extinguished, they were used atmospherically: darkness and half-light gave the illusion of vast spaces, while spots picked out the action.

All these steps and platforms and the gangway were to accommodate Reinhardt's crowd, and it was his crowd-work that everybody remembered first. For the London production he had recruited a regiment of R.A.D.A. students, with bevies of boy scouts to swell the number. From the very beginning, even against the towering black palace with its great bronze doors, it was the crowd that seized the imagination, as the *Telegraph* reported: "Moans and cries and shouts set the air throbbing, and crowd upon crowd of people surges in, and there the light breaks upon them, and they fall down suppliant and stretch out their hands, a whole nation of them, to one man – white-robed, bronze-breastplated – standing high above them, calm and stately, god-like".[14] *The Times* wrote with awe of the crowd's "animation and variety, its headlong rushes, its air of being some huge living organism,"[15] and when in Germany Martin-Harvey had seen its first entrance, he had found it to be one of the most thrilling *coups de théâtre* he had ever seen.[16]

The British critics were not always willing to be overwhelmed, and wrote defensively about the unaccustomed clamour: had not Sophocles managed with a chorus of only fifteen? The *Telegraph* decided that Reinhardt had not solved the problem of an Ancient Greek tragic chorus in the modern theatre, and thought that sometimes the crowd was simply in the way: "After all, we do not want pageantry intruding into Sophocles." The *Morning Post* also took an academic position: in his search after realism, Reinhardt seemed to have lost sight of the stage illusion, and the effect of "women rushing round and round in their frenzy" was more painful than it was effective; the attention was "constantly diverted by incursions first from one quarter and then from another"; and it concluded that "there is no reason why tragedy should be dull, but it must be calm and serene."[17] The established concepts of decorum in classical tragedy had clearly been undermined by all the movement, and for *The Nation* what the reviewer called the crowd's "well-schooled zeal of a Prussian regiment" lacked both dignity and delicacy.[18] *The Observer* was specific about an animated Oedipus: "His rushing down into the stalls to lug up the steps and fling upon the ground the reluctant shepherd was well nigh disastrous . . . And his final exit by groping and staggering through the audience . . . let down the last tremendous moment of the tragedy."[19] In *Punch*, Hazelden drew a picture of the terrible predicament that awaited the unfortunate spectator who should arrive late and be overtaken by a forest of Theban spears as he ran down the aisle.

Punch was also drawing attention to another element in this *Oedipus:* the way in which the audience itself was made use of. It is no doubt true that the Oedipus myth is dead, and that the ritual and metaphysical experience of the original cannot be revived, as Stan-

18   Sophocles' *Oedipus Rex* at Covent Garden, London, in 1912, with Sir John Martin-Harvey as Oedipus and design by Ernst Stern.

islaw Witkiewicz and others have contended.[20] The German audiences in their semicircle may have felt they were part of the action of the play, but they could share none of the American critic Francis Fergusson's "ritual expectancy" (*The Idea of the Theater* (1949), ch. 1). Nevertheless, Reinhardt was determined to overwhelm the senses of the spectator, perhaps in the hope that he might thereby capture his feelings and intelligence at least. The method he adopted was one of "*Sprengung des Bühnenrahmens*," extending the action past the footlights, "bursting out of the frame." Huntly Carter reported that "the actors do really move among the audience, there playing out their little drama in the midst of their fellow-men, just as the great drama is played every day of our life on earth,"[21] and we saw that even Oedipus himself, in his eagerness to learn what the shepherd could tell him, had hurled himself from the stage and through the audience. *The Observer*, very conscious of the proscenium arch and its needs, considered this to be a dangerous trick, since "it brings the picture out of the frame" and "checked the art of this tragedy again and again," but it could not deny that the rush of the crowd "swept the audience into the movement and produced an overwhelming impression of one's being part of the excited crowd." The *Telegraph* was more aware that "the coming and going of character after character through the ranks of the audience was a device from Berlin, not Athens," but concluded that, with "no curtain, no footlights, no orchestra . . . The modern convention by which a play is seen only like a picture in a frame was therefore abolished. We saw much of the *Oedipus* as you see the action of everyday life passing beside you and about you." The correspondent was not to know that within a few years "the device from Berlin" was to become a commonplace in the idiom of the modern theatre.

For the rest, Reinhardt simply used his skills and perception as a master craftsman. If the audience could not acquire a Greek point of view, if the foundation of the play was nowadays "incredible and absurd," to *The Times* this mattered "not a jot":

The tremendous dramatic impact and momentum of the thing were all there, the tragic irony, the sense of doom. As the crowd raised their white arms – a sea of white arms it was – in agonised supplication, we felt their agony. When they ran huddling in confusion before the door *on the other side* of which (O Hugo! O Maeterlinck!) such dread things were happening, we shared their anticipatory, conjectural terror.

Nor was Jocasta neglected. The *Telegraph* had:

It was not till Jocasta found her fears all true, and truth worse than she feared, when she gave a terrible low cry, and cowered and hid her face, when she tried to kiss him who still knew nothing, and could not, and rushed away, that she dominated the scene.

And all this before what *The Times* called "the crowning horror, the physical abomination of the hanged Jocasta and the sightless Oedipus, his eye-sockets streaming with gore."

Oedipus's final exit was unforgettable. He used the broad central gangway through the house, groping his way with blinded eyes through the audience, seen against the long drawn-out cry heard from the back of the empty stage. J. T. Grein in *The Sunday Times* complained that this was not Sophocles' ending, and believed that the Greek portals must close on the King "to indicate the total eclipse of the man and his career"[22] – but Grein may have forgotten that Oedipus had yet to journey to Colonus. However that may be, Martin-Harvey knew directly of the power of the Reinhardt exit and recorded that he had seen "some members of the audience who, in terror, have hidden their eyes" as he groped his way past them.[23]

Was this Greek tragedy? The debate raged on, and Richard Bentley's jibe at Pope's *Homer* was recalled: "It is a pretty performance, Herr Reinhardt, but you must not call it Sophocles." The grave figures of the Attic stage, the solemn distancing of the classical style, were quite lost: Greek restraint was compromised totally. But the *Telegraph* had a flash of unexpected insight, that this play had a "power of affectionate sympathy," and that Oedipus was "a most human king." Now that note of humanity had never before been struck, such a comment never heard. And when it came down to it, any comparison with the world-famous version by the great Mounet-Sully at the Comédie-Française was distinctly in Reinhardt's favour, whose theatre was by contrast "eloquent of doom and destiny."[24] The *Spectator* might consider Reinhardt's directorial hand too heavily Teutonic and vulgarized,[25] and Granville-Barker (who coached Lillah McCarthy in her part as Jocasta) might have preferred "more philosophy."[26] But perhaps in such a debate we should allow Gilbert Murray, scholar of the Greek theatre, almost the last word. He met head on the charge that the production was "unGreek":

By "Greek" we normally mean classical or fifth-century Greek. Now the *Oedipus* story itself is not Greek in that sense. It is pre-Greek; it belongs to the dark regions of pre-Hellenic barbarism. It struck one of the ancient Greek commentators, for instance, by its "senseless and bestial cruelty." Oedipus is pre-Hellenic; Sophocles is Greek. In the production ought we to represent the age of Sophocles or that of Oedipus? The point is arguable, and I have my own view about a middle course; but he who insists on keeping to the age and style of Sophocles must also insist on dressing Macbeth in Elizabethan ruffles.

Professor Reinhardt was frankly pre-Hellenic, partly Cretan and Mycen-aean, partly Oriental, partly – to my great admiration – merely savage. The half-naked torch-bearers with loin-cloths and long black hair made my heart leap with joy. There was real early Greece about them, not the Greece of the schoolroom or the conventional art studio.[27]

We might even conclude that the production was neither early nor late Greek, but mature Reinhardt.

7   The baroque spectacles

Reinhardt's giant productions of Gothic flavour are thought of as his indulgent spectacles for the masses. We should bear in mind, however, the comment of William Poel, the English director who relentlessly pressed Shakespeare's original staging on a reluctant public, when he actually praised *Das Mirakel* (*The Miracle*) for giving "practical shape on a large scale to the principle of Elizabethan staging."[1] If the conjunction of Shakespeare and the Globe with Reinhardt and Olympia boggles the mind a little, we should not forget that Reinhardt was the man who could both produce Germany's most sensitive Shakespeare and organize the Salzburg Festival.

Two of these Gothic plays, *Jedermann* (*Everyman*) after 1920 and *Das grosse Welttheater* (*The Great Theatre of the World*) after 1922, became his Salzburg Festival plays, and marked the pinnacle of his collaboration with the poet Hugo von Hofmannsthal. This great festival set the modern standard for occasions involving huge audiences. Such subsequent festivals as those at Malvern and Canterbury in 1929 acknowledge their conception to Reinhardt's work at Salzburg,[2] and these in turn became the models for the dozens of drama festivals we know in Britain, Europe and America today. Those interested in the theatre and the arts nowadays have many opportunities to come together in pleasant surroundings for several days rather than a few hours.

The ambitious purpose behind this kind of work was to encourage the participation of audiences. In an interview given in 1914, Reinhardt suggested that "in everyone is hidden something of an actor."[3] From the time of the first production of *Everyman* on 1 December 1911 at the Circus Schumann in Berlin and of *The Miracle* on 23 December that same year in London's Olympia, Reinhardt was thinking of a drama "for the people," as these unusual sites suggest. *The Miracle* transformed Olympia into a cathedral and its audience into a congregation. The Grosses Schauspielhaus in Berlin had formerly been the Circus Schumann, and the opening of that vast "Theatre of the Five Thousand" in 1919 was part of the same design, a circus for democracy. The Salzburg Festival, initiated the next year against local opposition with the help of Hofmannsthal, Richard Strauss, then director of the Vienna Opera, and Bruno Walter, director of the Vienna Philharmonic, was to be another and greater Oberammergau. When *Everyman* was played in the Domplatz, the cathedral square in Salzburg, criers from the church towers turned the whole city into a ritual theatre and the visitors into its communicants. Awakened from the eaves, even the pigeons seemed to be part of the plan. Reinhardt was delighted, and wrote in 1924, "All traffic comes to a halt, and the whole city listens and watches breathlessly."[4] When other productions of *Everyman* spilled into the Austrian villages, when in America the play was presented in modern dress and Reinhardt prepared plans for an all-black production, the impulse was the same.

The festival plays called for a special dramaturgy: a fusion of words and music, of acting and dancing – indeed, a fusion of all the arts in the best symbolist tradition. While the subjects represented a return to a popular, medieval simplicity and clarity, they were also an attempt to revive a ritual drama for modern times. In the view of H. I. Pilikian, it was a return to "pure theatre in the most archetypal sense," for he believed that Reinhardt was drawn to the sensuous quality of Catholic rites and Gregorian chants.[5] It was more: in 1903 Hofmannsthal had published an essay entitled, "The stage as dream image," and it was with something of the vision of poetic drama that the poet and the director approached their task.

At the time of the first production of *Everyman* in Hofmannsthal's lyrical version of irregular couplets, the author believed that he was restoring a play to the German repertory that should by rights have been part of it.[6] The idea was readily accepted. Reinhardt's production had a fair success in Berlin in 1911; it travelled to Frankfurt-on-Main and Budapest in 1912, and returned to Berlin in 1914. But it was not until 1920 that it acquired a world fame that made it one of the most remarkable events of this century. In that year it was chosen as the Salzburg Festival centrepiece; first it was a stopgap because of its simplicity and because it would be immediately understandable to all classes of playgoer,[7] and then it was continued for eighteen festivals because of its popularity; it is still playing in Salzburg every year. It had the clarity of a medieval woodcut, and kept the original story-line, in which Everyman is summoned by Death and makes frantic attempts to find someone to go with him. Yet Hofmannsthal saw the play as more than an allegory of life: it was more a mixture of reality and dream. In order to indicate the difference, Michael Hamburger quotes Hofmannsthal himself: "From this dream I rise and step over into that other dream which is called human world and

19   Hofmannsthal's *Everyman* in Salzburg, 1920, showing the cathedral
setting for the banquet scene; costume by Alfred Roller.

human life."[8] The poet's style and Reinhardt's direction kept the play in this limbo between fantasy and reality.

The Salzburg *Everyman* lapsed in 1921, and then in 1926 continued annually until 1937. Design was by Alfred Roller, the costumes by Ernst Stern and the music by Einar Nilson. From 1920 to 1921 and from 1926 to 1932, Everyman was played by Moissi, followed in 1932–34 by Hartmann, and in 1935–37 by Attila Hörbiger. Over the years, Beauty, Everyman's mistress, was played successively by Leopoldine Konstantin, Johanna Terwin and Dagny Servaes. Other important names became associated with the Salzburg roles: Werner Krauss as Death, Helene Thimig as Good Works and then in 1931 as Faith, Heinrich George, then Oskar Homolka, as Mammon, and Frieda Richard as Everyman's Mother.

All these characters had the strength of their simplicity. The Thin and the Fat Cousins were developed for comedy, and Hofmannsthal introduced Mammon as a new character to emphasize a more contemporary concern with material acquisitiveness. Everyman himself was developed as a wealthy burgher living a life of pleasure, a theme stressed by his devout old mother's anxiety about his soul and by his own lack of sympathy with a debtor who is dragged away to prison, leaving a wife in tears with her children at her skirts. Such detail of performance was always being extended or improved, and even as late as 1927 Reinhardt added a new conclusion to the play by having Everyman's funeral followed by a pathetic little procession of mourners consisting of his mother, his mistress and one or two others.[9] This was afterwards omitted.

Produced in the Domplatz with the consent of the Archbishop, the play's setting before Salzburg Cathedral lent a special character to the production, and Reinhardt seized the spatial opportunities offered. The performance itself took place on a platform set before the cathedral doors, but the sense that the action extended well beyond the stage proper was encouraged by every possible device. Actors made their entrances from neighbouring squares and Everyman himself entered from the audience, where he had been sitting quietly in a dark cloak. Concealed entrances around the platform permitted sudden appearances from heaven or hell, as when the Devil sprang up from the spectators' benches, or angels appeared from the cathedral. Not only were the choir and the organ heard from within, but at carefully timed moments Reinhardt had the bells of other churches rung as well. When the moment came, mysterious voices called Everyman to his death from church towers and steeples far in the distance, and were even carried on the wind from the Hohensalz-

20 Hofmannsthal's *Everyman* in Salzburg, 1926, with Alexander Moissi as Everyman and Luis Rainer as Death.

burg, the wooded fortress that loomed over the city. Hofmannsthal described the effect:

The cries uttered by invisible spirits to warn Everyman of his approaching death sounded not only from the church before whose façade the stage had been built, but from all the church-towers of the city, as twilight deepened about the five thousand spectators. One of these criers had been placed in the highest tower of a medieval castle, built far above the city, and his voice sounded, weird and ghostly, about five seconds after the others, just as the first rays of the rising moon fell cold and strange from the high heavens on the hearts of the audience.[10]

All commentators remarked this magical use of natural light, as day-light changed to sunset and then to a night lit by flaming torches, in time for the gentle entrance of Faith in the habit of a nun from the darkness of the cathedral, and for the voice of Everyman as he spoke his Paternoster.

If the movements and gestures of the actors achieved a puppet-like angularity reminiscent of a medieval woodcut, the major impact came, however, not from style, but from the orchestration of the action. Thus, the *Regiebücher* from Salzburg[11] and the promptbook for the Hollywood production of 1940[12] supply some of the details of what happened at such a critical moment as when Everyman was finally summoned to his death.

The moment of the reappearance of Death at the end of the play was first prepared by business that grew more and more animated and louder and louder as Everyman and his companions in revelry, the Fat Cousin, the Thin Cousin and *"Buhlshaft,"* his mistress, reached a climax of singing and drinking. Everyman and the girl were at the centre of roisterous laughter and general embracing when "he clasps her without warning and kisses her on the mouth. She frees herself and firmly gives him a resounding box on the ear. He is painfully astonished, holds his cheek. Laughter all around." Meanwhile the Thin Cousin "begins a canon, which is taken up by the others as he swings his guitar like a bell." And Reinhardt actually composed a line or two to enhance the effect he was about to spring:

> Oh, how well I feel at nightfall, feel at nightfall, feel at nightfall,
> When the bells toll rest and quiet, Bimbam, Bimbam, Bimbam, Bimbam, Bum.

What they sang was heavily ironic, for at that moment "the dull toll-ing of a bell" was actually heard.

The sound of the tolling was to be "celestial," that is, "heard from a distance, sounding from high above, increasingly severe and omi-nous." But only Everyman heard it, as the audience saw because he set his glass down and pushed it away from him, listening with a "terrified" expression as the singing continued. He rose slowly, first looking at the others to see whether they too had heard the sound:

> What bell is that? It can mean nothing good,
> Methinks, so loud and fearsome is the sound!

The girl asked, "What bell?", hearing nothing. Everyman's voice rose to a shout and brought the song to a stop:

> Now terror strikes my heart! Why toll that bell
> At this hour?

Now in the silence everyone heard the tolling bell. Everyman cried out and his mistress tried to calm him as everyone laughed at his fears. The girl, full of life, called for the song to continue, but Everyman, "white as death," spoke through a "dry throat": "Now I will never hear it again." It was at this point that the audience heard his name called again and again across the city: "Everyman! Everyman!"

Reinhardt's control of sight, sound and space in this production produced a strong response from the large crowd of spectators, and the Archbishop himself was moved to tears – he pressed Reinhardt's hand after the performance and declared that the play was worth more than a sermon. But not everyone was as pleased. Granville-Barker saw it in 1936 and recalled one of Poel's frequent revivals of the English version, done more simply. Granville-Barker wrote in a letter to Harcourt Williams,

We went to Salzburg for our holiday. The best of the music magnificent. Reinhardt – I make reserves, the *Everyman*: very dashing in its way. But all sin and no redemption! The banquet magnificent, but the Mass a foozle. No; that is unjust. The thing is very well done and yet – and yet! At no moment did I want to go on my knees. And I could hardly keep from it when Old Poel first did it – the real thing; not Hofmannsthal – in the St George's Hall years ago.[13]

That at bottom was the criticism of a purist anxious to preserve the past.

The poet Else Lasker-Schüler disliked Hofmannsthal's work generally, and wrote to Herwarth Walden, editor of *Die Aktion*, the expressionist periodical:

I've been to see Everyman or is it called All-Sorts? I think it is called All-Sorts for Everyman or Everyman for All-Sorts. Come in, ladies and gentlemen, to the giant Punch and Judy show. Where did it all come from? I think from the stables, Herwarth . . . The performance of *Jedermann* is an unartistic act, a shameful one . . . Life and death, sin and judgment, Heaven and Hell – all are degraded to a spectacle, like those elephants and Arab horses decorated with ribbons and trinkets, yet not even for the delight of children in that case, but for the edification of a rich sensation-hungry public.[14]

Hofmannsthal's sincerity was never in doubt, but this comment expressed the discomfort felt by a fellow poet when she witnessed his attempt to make himself a more public poet.

The play had a surprisingly indifferent success in New York in 1941, and Brooks Atkinson also found the production sensational:

> Taken out of its period, *Everyman* seems to modern ears uncomfortably like an immorality play . . . Everyman manages to have a lot of cake and eat it too. He is rich and sinful; he . . . holds iniquitous wassail with his mistress and revellers. Although an eleventh hour conversion gets him into heaven with envious alacrity, it takes a keener eye than this theatregoer has to detect any improvement in his moral character.[15]

Atkinson wanted a more primitive, authentic treatment, and his criticism was that of the puritan troubled by a popular performance of what he took to be sacred material. Nevertheless, none of these critics could deny that between them Hofmannsthal and Reinhardt had performed a considerable service to the theatre by mounting a previously remote drama and making it an unforgettable event accessible to thousands of modern playgoers.

Enough has been written about *The Miracle*[16] – and its New York *Regiebuch* has been available for many years – for us to consider chiefly the dramatic and theatrical issues of the production. Its success at the box-office helped it to travel blithely, in spite of its sheer bulk, like any other popular Reinhardt enterprise. The British promoter, C. B. Cochran, had seen the Berlin *Oedipus* and hired London's largest covered space, Olympia, for Reinhardt. The hall was to seat 8,000 spectators; the play was to be chosen later. So it was that London was the first to witness *The Miracle* in 1911, but thereafter it was recreated in Vienna (1912), Leipzig, Dresden, Elberfeld, Breslau, Cologne, Prague and Frankfurt (1913), Hamburg and Karlsruhe (1914), Berlin (1914 and 1915), and Sweden and Bucharest (1917). A new production was presented by Morris Gest in New York in 1924, and this toured the United States until 1930. The Salzburg Festival enjoyed it in 1925, and Budapest, Prague and Vienna had it again in 1927. Finally, Cochran brought it back to London in 1932, this time to the Lyceum. (It was made into a film in 1959, with Carroll Baker as the Nun.) The early productions were designed by Stern, and a solemn and seductive music was composed and conducted by Engelbert Humperdinck, composer of *Hansel and Gretel*.

The gentle story of the nun who falls from grace and the Madonna

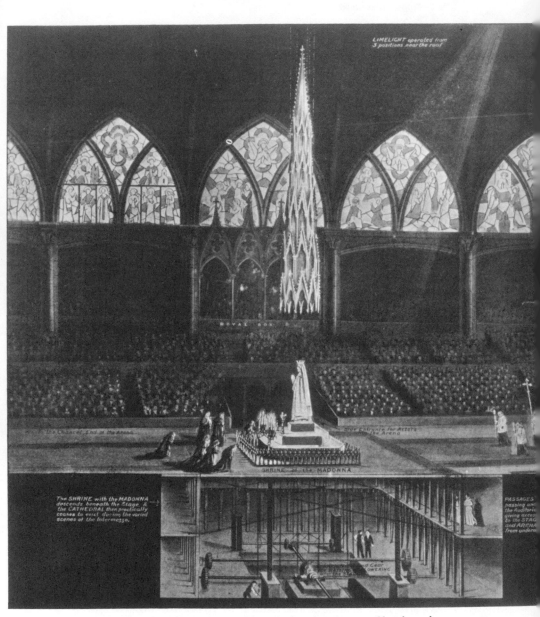

Within the image, the following labels appear:

LIMELIGHT operated from
3 positions near the roof

ROYAL BOX

...to the Chancel End in the Arena

Side Entrance for Actors
to the Arena

SHRINE of the MADONNA

The SHRINE with the MADONNA
descends beneath the Stage &
the CATHEDRAL then practically
ceases to exist during the varied
scenes of the Intermezzo.

PASSAGES
passing under
the Auditoria
giving access
to the STAGE
and ARENA
from underneath

...d Gear
...WERING

21 Vollmoeller's *The Miracle* at Olympia, London, in 1911. Sketches of
the design by Ernst Stern.

Rails on which the Hill & Trees are wheeled into the Arena

...sition occupied by the HILL and TREES later on

The great SLIDING DOORS are here shown
as open to exhibit the SCENE to better advantage, the smaller CATHEDRAL DOORS which
slide into the larger ones are marked X

who takes her place until her penitent return was adapted as a production scenario by Karl Vollmoeller from Maeterlinck's *Sister Beatrice*, one of that dramatist's more romantic subjects, idealizing the triumph of the spirit over the flesh. The style was quite unnaturalistic: indeed, John Palmer pointed out that it was no accident that the production coincided with the publication of two key books of the symbolist movement in English, Gordon Craig's *On the Art of the Theatre* and Yeats's *Plays for an Irish Theatre*.[17] But *Sister Beatrice* had recently been played in the tiny Court Theatre in 1909; now Maeterlinck's simple material had to be swollen to fill no less a place than Olympia. What is more, Olympia was not available for rehearsal until December, although the first night was to be 23 December, so that the production had only three and a half weeks to make ready. It had to close soon after to make way for the *Daily Mail* Ideal Home Exhibition.

When Stern first saw Olympia he described it as "a railway station of iron girders and glass full of motor cars."[18] The floor space was 440 by 250 feet, four times that of the Albert Hall, and its roof rose 100 feet high. The great size of the place was the source of most of the dramatic problems, but Reinhardt determined to take advantage of one quality that size could bring: in the manner of the Greek and Elizabethan theatres, he would place his audience at the centre of the action by turning the building itself into the cathedral where the play would begin and end, arranging the spectators on each side to seem like a congregation. In effect, Olympia was to become a twelfth-century Gothic cathedral, its architect Hermann Derburg. To assure the effect, there were to be six-foot-high gold lamps, a towering gold canopy over the Madonna, and stained-glass windows, including a circular one of 50 feet in diameter, larger than the original in Cologne and three times the size of the rose window in Notre Dame.

Whether the spectator felt like a member of a congregation remains uncertain, but effects of space were certainly achieved. The correspondents for *The Daily Telegraph* and *The Times* between them gave an ecstatic account of the opening scene:

Suddenly from afar off comes the sound of a massive bell, solemnly tolling. The effect is electrical. In the centre of a cathedral nave, as if by some magic it has been caught up from the depths of the crypt below, appears the figure of the Madonna, garbed in a vestment heavy with gold and precious stones . . . Slowly the lights gather strength; dotted here and there on the stone floor are seen a few stray worshippers upon their knees, reciting in muttered tones an Ave Maria.

Then the great west doors, 70 feet wide and 100 feet high, three times the size of those in Cologne Cathedral, were thrown open and, headed

by an ecclesiastical procession of unexampled splendour, a vast con-
course of people poured down the slopes of a hill outside in order to
celebrate the Virgin's fête.

So great is the distance that at first they look no bigger than dwarfs or pig-
mies, fantastic little figures dancing on the green sward. Little by little, as
they advance towards the figure of the Madonna, they assume the proportions of men and women.

So the cathedral was crowded with people all inspired with joy. And
then the great space emptied:

Slowly as this pitch has been reached, it as slowly subsides. The nuns go
one way, the people another; and at last the great church is empty save for
the gleaming statue in its blazing robe and crown, and for one solitary nun,
to whom is left the care of it – with the keys of the cathedral. Those keys she
uses before she should. Outside the great west door there is piping and
singing. The children are there, and children she cannot resist. She lets them
in, plays with them, dances with them, and the love of playing and dancing
gets hold of her. For with the children she has let in someone else, the gay,
sinister figure of a wandering *Spielmann* [minstrel], whose pipe is the call of
the blood.[19]

For exterior scenes, a grassy mound with three trees was wheeled
in through the doors a few yards up the nave (the same device was
managed better with electricity in New York in 1924). "Once a cathedral, always a cathedral," was the comment in *Punch*,[20] and the
attempt to sustain the initial realism was abandoned. Then Reinhardt had 40,000 tons of earth excavated for a trap in the centre of the
arena, using half a million bricks to support the walls of the pit
beneath, and through this trap he elevated the interior scenes.
Norman Bel Geddes, designer for the New York production, considered that this worked well if each scene dissolved smoothly into the
next. The cathedral, he argued, "must plausibly become – right before
the eyes of the audience and without so much as a blackout – a pri-
meval forest, a banquet hall, a wedding chapel, a setting for a black
mass, a great throne room for the coronation of an empress, a public
square, a stable interior, a roadway through a wintry forest, and
finally, a cathedral again."[21] By then any realism had doubtless already
dissolved into dream and fantasy, and the *tableaux vivants* and the
dumb-show of such scenes as the Banquet of Brigands and the
Inquisition were quite acceptable.

Nor was the set realistic. Stern described the pointed arches of the
cathedral interior as "decorated with masses of tracery soaring
upwards. Improbable and fantastically involved arabesques curled
into flowers, leaves and fruit which, on closer examination, proved
to be grotesquely distorted masks." And although he had the cos-

tumes made of authentic materials – real metal for armour, real leather, real silk and fur, and the Madonna's robes actually sprayed with concrete to give them the quality of stone – he did not consider them to be realistic:

The costumes were as fantastic as the architecture, like something out of a feverish dream. The actresses wore enormously high steeple hats. The actors wore massive headgear from which stiff folds of cloth shot out like flames. And the leg-of-mutton sleeves were fantastic, more like balloons, whilst the trains of the women were tremendously long and ornate. To add to the fantasy there was a vast amount of scalloping which hung down magnificently rounded, pointed, jagged, from every seam. And on their feet these men and women, dressed like Harlequins and parakeets, wore boots and shoes with excessively long pointed toes.

And then in contrast to this overdressing was the revelation described in the text of bosom, belly, leg and thigh. The fashion was devilish, grotesque and mocking, recklessly extravagant and exaggerated. It grinned, so to speak; it mocked; it stuck out its tongue at the prudish. And the colours were daz-

22   Vollmoeller's *The Miracle* at Olympia, London, in 1911, with Natasha Trouhanowa as the Nun in the scene of the Robber Baron's banquet.

zling. The scallops and hangings twisted and twirled in the dance of life like the flames of hell.[22]

Stern was sceptical about the play itself, and called it "that ephemeral airy-fairy confection of sugar candy."[23] This opinion may account for the violent, baroque images he invented, and he was no doubt right to think that his exaggerated approach to the costumes helped the actors to appear appropriately larger than life.

The critics remarked the effects of harmony in the colours of the costumes and lighting, especially of orange and rose tints, and the *Regiebuch*, indeed, contains an unusual "colour key" to each scene, showing where greens and blues must change to blues and violets, or to vermilion and gold, and so on. These special effects were an extension of the symbolist impulse to express the special moods of the play. One such effect was a grim representation of the Inquisition in which the Nun was tried as a witch by ghastly hooded figures who brought her to trial riding on a rack through a maddened mob. Another was the burning of the royal palace in the scene of the Coronation: when the Nun danced before the King, the streaming ribbons of the maskers were to appear to catch alight from the torches, resulting in an inferno of smoke and flame. This effect was accomplished by a curtain of steam and long yellow streamers blown up from below by a current of air. Huntly Carter saw how this was done:

Forty-seven electric fans drove up the yellow silken ribbons upon which the light from the forty arc lamps beat. The shrieks of the revellers filled up the intervals of the fiery effects as they made themselves felt in the conflagration overhead. For some moments we stood in the midst of blinding lights, flashing flames, and crashing winds. Then the bell rang and there was the silence and darkness of death.[24]

The *Telegraph* reported that the scene was cut by the London County Council because they feared the fire might be mistaken for the real thing.

None of the central scenes, however, were in any way realistic. Every detail carried a suggestion, usually of something outrageously grotesque, appropriately accented by effects of music and light. The scene of the Wedding of the Nun and the Prince was especially bizarre: the bells sounded like cow-bells, a major-domo wore religious robes with a fool's cap, acolytes carried Hallowe'en lanterns instead of candles, girl pages carried trays with their heads sticking out through holes, bridesmaids on broomsticks were really men wearing beautiful masks, the groom's men riding on hobby horses were girls in masks also, an aged witch led in the bride, and last in the crazy procession came the Spielmann dressed as a bishop with an enormous mitre and donkey's ears. With his eternal pipe, this Spielmann, played by Max Pallenberg, was an inspired stroke in the play: like Mephistopheles in *Faust,* he was always hovering near, first playing his eerie pipe on the hill outside the cathedral, then hopping, dancing, grimacing with the Nun wherever she went, bringing disaster to all who had dealings with her.

All this called for production on a vast scale: 2,000 actors, a choir of 500, an orchestra of 200 with a great organ. Apart from calling for a mastery of all the arts of the theatre and a special gift of marshalling crowds, the production demanded an organizing genius to oversee the multitude of details – Reinhardt used call-boys on bicycles to race along Olympia's endless corridors to call individual groups of players into action. But of course the sheer size of the actual performance brought with it unique difficulties for the success of the whole. *Punch* was the most scathing about the excessive patterns of movement required, and thought that Olympia was "perhaps a little roomy" when only one actor was wanted: "It needs a circle of limelight (thrown upon her from a hanging platform in the roof) to enable the Knight, stationed outside the great west doors, to locate the object of his passion; but how he contrived to set a precise value on her charms without the aid of field-glasses, I cannot hope to guess."[25] The reviewer did not remember seeing before "so lengthy a body of *religieuses* executing so lengthy a movement at the double." The *Athenaeum* also took up this theme, suggesting that Reinhardt was "at the mercy of the size of his medium. When his stage is not full it looks empty; when scenes essential to the plot, but requiring only a few characters, are played in his huge theatre, they seem to drag and to be dwarfed by the tableaux in which masses of people take part."[26] And this and other critics found that the pace of the production also suffered from the excess of space: the tempo dragged and longueurs resulted from the time lost in filling the great acting areas. And there were inevitably moments, or so *The Times* reported, "when the spectacle is not satisfactory from this or that particular spot." It was the problem of focus that plagues all arena productions, "the difficulty of taking in the spectacle as a whole and the effort of trying to see in two or three directions at once." Reinhardt would cure this only when he moved the play inside a normal proscenium theatre.

The Morris Gest production of *The Miracle* at the Century Theatre, New York, in 1924 solved the problem while remaining equally impressive with its statistics – the newspapers reported joyfully that there were 3,000 costumes made by 100 seamstresses, 5,800 lb of lampblack and 2 tons of stage snow; the cathedral inside the theatre was 200 feet long, 120 feet wide and 110 feet high, for which 871 drawings were made with 44 wiring diagrams; 300 workers toiled for five months, using 1,000,000 feet of wood; the cost of the production was $400,000, of which $100,000 was for the set, and so on. A scenic miracle was judged to have been performed in the theatre: "[There were] soaring columns and groined arches filling the stage and masking the interior of the house as far back as the balcony . . . The proscenium arch became the choir with the high altar set in the midst . . . The theatre has been literally turned into a cathedral, not a mere contrivance of canvas and paint."[27] The effect was completed by the sounds of sacred music as the audience came in, and ushers in nun's wimples showed them to their pews in a dim religious light.

The New York critics were enraptured, some considering the production to be the greatest ever seen in America.[28] But perhaps the use of nuns as ushers had gone too far; perhaps there is a limit to what the arts of the theatre can achieve; for rumblings of discontent were also heard. The *Tribune* confessed that "before the evening was over [the play] had assumed a little of the monotony which sometimes afflicts the greatest of pantomimes"; the production was "tediously complete." In *The New Republic* Stark Young wondered whether there was really anything behind the performance. And a few years later Percy Hammond in the *Herald Tribune* would employ the term "Barnum and Bailey" to describe Reinhardt's aesthetic achievement.[29]

When the play was revived by Cochran at the Lyceum in London in 1932 ("Traffic jams in the Strand": *The Observer*), the set was by Oscar Strnad, the costumes were by Oliver Messel and the choreography was by Leonide Massine, who also played the Spielmann. Again the attempt was made to turn the theatre into a piece of cathedral and the corridors into cloisters. The *Telegraph* reported that the familiar interior of the Lyceum had completely vanished, and that "wherever the eye wandered it met the semblance of weathered stone."[30] However, *The Times* was troubled by "the interruption to design of a rectangular proscenium opening" and "the presence of our alien selves."[31] And, in spite of programme-selling nuns, costumes of the customary splendour, an exquisite Tilly Losch (actually more at home in the world than in the church) as the Nun, and a new scene in which she was scourged and crucified (withdrawn after two weeks because it was physically painful to the audience), the voices raised in criticism grew louder.

The *Telegraph* questioned the taste of "playing to the gallery with the Crucifix," and considered that having the sacred and profane battle for mastery in "an orgy of symbolism" was "a dream to box the compass of any Freudian." *The Times* had "a pervasive sense of something strained and false and theatrical":

A pageant *The Miracle* is, and one could praise its splendours with a less divided mind if it claimed to be no more. But it does lay claim to a spiritual beauty not of this world, and the claim is false. The cathedral is impressive if we forget cathedrals; the ceremonies if we forget their original. The play is full of ingenious substitutes for truth which, like the electric bulbs that do service for candles, are enemies of the spirit while decorative of the substance.

That the production touched the uneasy borderland in which theatre and religion meet was the new source of criticism. Ivor Brown in *The Observer* believed this to be "dangerous country," and finally wondered whether it were all worthwhile: " 'Impressive but irrelevant' as the schoolboy said when they beat him for an uncommitted crime."[32]

So it was that this extraordinary piece of Reinhardt's theatre passed into the record books. It was probably a case of sublime overreaching, but seen as a test of all the new devices of the modern theatre put to work on audiences of many different kinds, it would not be quite lost in oblivion.

With the possible exception of Franz Werfel's *The Eternal Road*, produced at the Manhattan Opera House, New York, in 1937 to commemorate the persecution of the Jews through history, the last of Reinhardt's great pageants was *The Salzburg Great Theatre of the World*. In many ways more complex and sophisticated than either *Everyman* or *The Miracle*, it was, like these, an allegory and a morality play. It was adapted by Hofmannsthal from Calderón's *El gran teatro del mundo* of 1649, itself a unique attempt to bring to life on a stage the medieval image of *theatrum mundi*, the concept by which the world, its people and their ways reflect the purposes of God, and by which providence can be seen at work in the affairs of men and women.

Hofmannsthal's prefatory note to the publication of his version in 1922 may serve to introduce it:

Everyone knows that there is a spiritual drama by Calderón called *The Great Theatre of the World*. From this play the whole pivotal metaphor has been borrowed: that the World erects a stage on which men enact the play of life in the roles allotted to them by God; also the title of this play and the names of the six characters who represent human life – and that is the whole extent of the borrowing. Yet these constituents do not belong to the great Catholic poet as his invention, but are part of that treasury of myths and allegories which the Middle Ages shaped and bequeathed to later centuries.[33]

Hofmannsthal's motto for the play was "Do Right: Under God!" and the setting itself was intended to embody the idea that man is merely an actor on God's stage as "The Master" looks down. In the story, God orders the World to produce a play:

MASTER. The conduct and activity of men is worthy of a play for me. For this I have invited these guests of mine [the Prophets]. Now build us the stage and let the play begin.

WORLD. But I know nothing yet about it!

ANGEL. Call up now a crowd of unborn souls and clothe them with flesh; then He will give each one of them a destiny.[34]

Six such souls, created free, are then dressed to play the parts assigned and face their destiny. They are the King, robed in crown and mantle, Wisdom in the habit of a nun, the Rich Man in furs, the Farmer in rougher clothes, Beauty dressed as a court lady, and the Beggar. Only the Beggar refuses to accept what he is given: rags. This part was considerably developed from the more passive original of Calderón, where, as in the Bible, he is blessed merely because of his poverty; now he is the disinherited, clamouring for his rights. The Angel must intercede and explain that it is for each player to give meaning to his life: how does he know whether he has drawn Esau's part or Jacob's? When Death finally calls the players to leave the world's stage and discard their costumes, it will be the Beggar who leads them back to the Master.

This was the play that replaced the *Everyman* in Salzburg in 1922, and was performed in the old Kollegienkirche, a splendid, baroque, Jesuit church of the eighteenth century. Design was by Roller and the music, chiefly old Gregorian chants, by Einar Nilson. The Beggar was played by Moissi, with Helene Thimig as Wisdom. The production was revived in the Salzburg Festspielhaus in the summer of 1925, but the demand for *Everyman* displaced *The Great Theatre of the World* as the festival play in the following year. Reinhardt offered it to Berlin at the Deutsches Theater in 1933 as his very last production in that city, indeed in Germany, but such a play could not long survive the political atmosphere of the time.

The stage structure was conceived to convey the dual perspectives of the world and the spirit. Alfred Schwarz has pointed out that, while Hofmannsthal's characters are completely caught up in their earthly roles, the spectator always sees the two worlds of passing time and eternity, of play-acting and reality, spatially juxtaposed.[35] The *whole* stage of life is made visible, not merely a visible world haunted by an invisible order, as in *Everyman*. And Reinhardt's stage arrangements managed to make this work. Each character was led to a Gothic niche as if in some fifteenth-century tapestry, and the grace-ful Palladian proportions of the chancel with its high altar were adapted as acting areas. The altar was draped in scarlet, and the same colour was carried right round the church at a height of about fifteen feet. Before the altar was erected a platform the width of the church, and five steps had to be climbed to reach an upper platform. Rein-hardt thus planned his movements in the vertical as well as the hor-izontal. More, he placed his angels in the little loges set in the cupola at the end of the church. He had chosen to experiment with sound and vision as another spatial sensation for his audience, but this time one smaller in scale and under finer control than in his previous pag-eants.

Hofmannsthal's text provided many opportunities for Reinhardt and his players to improvise and extend the play's images and ideas. One such opportunity arose when the Beggar rebelled against his role and Reinhardt introduced a pantomime for which Eric Gort was asked to create a number of masks – "faces of people groping in the darkness of poverty, faces of men behind the gates of jails, faces of women worn out by hard work, peeping with narrow eyes out of the dusk of their dim lives."[36] This pantomime came close to Hof-mannsthal's own conception of poverty as a state of dispossession and disinheritance, "the threat of chaos to the world of order."[37]

We are fortunate to have Gort's first-hand description of Rein-hardt's improvisation at this moment in the play. After the Beggar was refused his request for a different dress, in despair he cried, "That anyone should be condemned to live like that, it's unthinka-ble!" With that, he sprang up and raised his arms in defiance, and this was the cue for a sequence of vivid, balletic impressions:

At this moment light vanishes and darkness fills the theatre. Out of this darkness, there rises slowly the fantastic vision of coming revolutions, of bloodshed and destruction. First a group of thirty dancers, wearing masks of various types, rushes across the stage. In a pantomime of growing vio-lence, green and yellowish faces emerge in glaring flashes of light. This dance rises to a horrible climax, gradually subsiding as another group of masks begins to make its appearance. Now pale, gray faces emerge from the pal-pitating darkness like foam on bubbling mud. They come on and on, men and women out of the slums, from poorhouses and jails, the dregs of human society, guilty and innocent, some in despair, some in defiance. They join in the mighty wave of hatred and violence, raising their arms to overthrow the order of the world. The dance once more rises to a climax, when sud-denly in the midst of the confusion, the image of the crucifix appears in a moonlike radiance. Hatred and violence pass away in view of this apparition of divine love and humility. This is the end of the pantomime.[38]

23 Hofmannsthal's *The Salzburg Great Theatre of the World* at the Festspielhaus, Salzburg, in 1925; design by Eduard Hütter and costume by Ernest de Weerth. With Lil Dagover as Beauty, Wilhelm Dieterle as the King, Helene Thimig as Wisdom, Oskar Homolka as the Rich Man and Luis Rainer as Death.

The choreography for this interlude was by Albert Talhoff.

Nevertheless, the one scene left in everyone's memory was the *danse macabre* with which Reinhardt introduced the final movement of the play. The Angel called to Death to stop the performance and take the players off one after the other, beginning with the King. Hofmannsthal's lines read,

ANGEL. The play already soon will reach its end;
Now call the actors, one by one, away!
DEATH (*advances from where he stands to the rim of the upper stage and calls loudly*).
You who have the role of the King, step off!
The part your play is over: leave the stage![39]

This gave Reinhardt the chance to make the part of Death not only more important than Hofmannsthal had conceived it, but as overwhelming to the imagination of the audience as it had been in *Everyman*. Reinhardt himself said the reason for the development was that the actor playing Death, Luis Rainer, was physically so lithe and rhythmical that he could build a whole *Totentanz*, dance of death, around him.[40]

Hofmannsthal reported that the scene was among the most impressive Reinhardt had ever created, so impressive that "a shudder, half sigh, half audible moan, ran through the audience crowded together in the twilight of the church, and for a moment it seemed as though the effect might be too much for their nerves." The poet's own description of the dance of death is worth reproducing in full:

The actor who played Death was very slender, with most expressive features, and a thorough athlete. During the play he had stood motionless as a statue on a high column covered with scarlet cloth. He and the angel who stood at a similar height opposite him might readily have been taken for part of the church's architecture.

At the moment when God gave him permission to take up his part in the action, he left his lofty perch and climbed soundlessly down by means of an invisible ladder concealed in the scarlet stuff. As he came, he beat with two long bone drumsticks upon a tiny drum fixed to the girdle of his costume. His costume was that of a Spanish cavalier, all black, and he walked with a strange, slim grace. The fearful rhythm of his drumming sounded from gongs and kettle drums hidden in the organ loft.

He came so to the first figure he had to summon, the King. Striding backward, his cavernous sockets fixed on the King, he compelled him by the power of his drum-beat to come down from his throne and to follow him step by step. But the power of the drum was such that the King was attracted and repelled by it at the same time. He walked no longer like a living being to the beat of an instrument. He walked as though his soul were no longer in his body, but in those drum-beats. Like a puppet hanging by strings, the

King followed the Drummer and jerked out mechanically the lines he had to say. So Death led him toward the audience; then, by the very strength of his drum, jerked him back and forth, and finally forced him into his place again.

Then Death took the next person – the Rich Man or Beauty – and did the same thing, forward and backward; and so, one after another, with all six figures. And during the sixfold repetition of his gruesome dance, the audience sat as though hypnotized and rooted to their seats.[41]

It is no small thing to spellbind an audience for the two or three hours of a performance, but with *The Salzburg Great Theatre of the World* the reports suggest that this was the case. And it is fitting to acknowledge, as Hofmannsthal did, that Reinhardt here managed to spellbind an unusually mixed audience, mixed in class and nationality, an audience ranging from Austrian peasants and their families to serious playgoers from as far away as America. The final achievement of Reinhardt's great festival productions was perhaps to find a way to realize his dream of a theatre for everyone. Or nearly everyone.

8   Reinhardt, man of the theatre

There is more to be said about the range of Reinhardt's work than space allows. His treatment of opera and operetta, a direct result of his concern for incidental music in drama, deserves attention, in particular his collaboration with Richard Strauss, and with Hofmannsthal as librettist, for *Der Rosenkavalier* in 1911 and *Ariadne auf Naxos* in 1912. In these Reinhardt brought a new image to modern opera, and in 1929 he dusted off Johann Strauss's *Die Fledermaus* and transformed it by the vitality of his production. There is also something to be said about Reinhardt's work as a film director, in particular of his casting of Warner Brothers' contract players for the film *A Midsummer Night's Dream* in 1935: Olivia de Havilland for Hermia, the boy Mickey Rooney for an elfin Puck and James Cagney for the part of Bottom, displaying the gangland confidence of *Public Enemy* (1931). In spite of the howls of the more scholarly critics, this production offered a first proof that the poetic stage and the modern screen need not be quite incompatible, and Robert Willson has made an amusing case for considering the chase through the wood as an extension of Frank Capra's kind of "screwball comedy" in *It Happened One Night* (1934), and the Pyramus and Thisbe scenes (with Bottom getting to the palace just in time) an analogy with the early helter-skelter rehearsal musicals of Busby Berkeley, like *42nd Street* (1933).[1]

However, Reinhardt is today chiefly remembered for his constant search for a functional playhouse, the right vehicle for the particular play he was directing, for the development of the playhouse and its technical advances, and for his methods of repertory and his ways of preparing and rehearsing a play. In summarizing Max Reinhardt's qualities as a practical man of the theatre, it is not easy to separate the technician from the artist. And as a director he was infinitely adaptable. Just as his many productions differed from one another, so his working approach differed from production to production. As time passed, he ensured that he had a choice of stage to work with, and in his time he claimed with pride that he had built or rebuilt no less than thirteen theatres, at one time operating ten of them in Berlin and Vienna simultaneously.[2] All were managed by his careful, but indispensable, brother Edmund, who not only controlled the books for the theatres, the company and the workshops, but also rented the accommodation and paid the servants.

The tiny cabaret theatres with which Reinhardt began his directing career in 1901 in Berlin, "Die Brille" ("The Spectacles") and "Schall und Rauch" ("Sound and Smoke") on the Unter den Linden, where he tried his hand with short realistic pieces, were not much bigger than a hotel room. These places at least offered the opportunity of intimate acting, and began to reveal an enduring principle, that the response of an audience varies in direct relationship with both the style of the play and the scale of the playhouse. A year later, "Schall und Rauch" was turned into his first proper theatre, the intimate Kleines Theater ("Little Theatre"). There, with plays like *Salomé* and *The Lower Depths,* he felt the strength of actor–audience proximity, something he was not to forget even after he had practised his art on a far larger scale.

Reinhardt adjusted his sights when he took over the larger Neues Theater on the Schiffbauerdamm in 1903. Lessing and Shaw, Schiller and Shakespeare now fell within his purview, and for two or three years he gave its stage no respite, keeping the Kleines Theater working alongside it. Then in 1905 Adolf L'Arronge, owner of the most cosmopolitan theatre in Berlin, the Deutsches Theater, established in 1883, offered Reinhardt the post of director, and this was to be the centre of his operations for sixteen years. He immediately began a process of rebuilding, adding a revolve to the stage and an apron to the forestage, making it serviceable for every kind of play that did not cater for a small, specialized audience or that had no need for the sweep of an arena. Within six months Reinhardt was in a position to buy this theatre for a million marks, and the lessee became the owner. With a comparatively young company, the Deutsches Theater became the scene of some of his best work: *The Merchant of Venice,* Hofmannsthal's *Oedipus and the Sphinx, Twelfth Night, The Robbers,* Grillparzer's *Medea, King Lear,* Nestroy's *Revolution in Krähwinkel, Faust,* all plays in the classical repertoire which enjoyed long runs in the early years.

Reinhardt had given up the Kleines Theater when he went to the Deutsches Theater, but he was quick to find another intimate house. This was the famous Kammerspiele ("chamber theatre," the name coined by Reinhardt himself) of 1906, the theatre which became the prototype for Strindberg's Kammarspel and chamber theatres all over Europe. Adapted from the tavern and dance-hall next door to the parent house, it was luxuriously appointed, panelled in oak with comfortable, red-leather armchairs and red walls. But its size was of first importance. The auditorium was no bigger than the stage itself, and there was no orchestra pit or prompt box to divide stage from audience. It seated only 292 people, and the front row was only three feet from the stage, so that players at the back were closer to the spectators than they had formerly been on an apron.

"Ever since I've been in the theatre," Reinhardt declared, "I wanted to pursue one definite purpose, and I've finally achieved it: to bring the actor and the spectator together – as close together as possible."[3] The Kammerspiele was Reinhardt's truly intimate theatre, in which a unique unity between stage and audience could be created. On the technical side, the acoustics and sightlines could not be faulted, and the focus of attention was everything an actor could ask. According to Siegfried Jacobsohn,[4] not a whisper was lost, and every detail was made to count. Reinhardt himself later thought that "the small size of the theatre, the proximity of the stage, the extra comfort of the seats, were all a mistake: the quality of an audience grows with its quantity."[5] However, everyone agreed that in the Kammerspiele Reinhardt had created "a jewel casket which should contain the more fragile or the more intimate of his creations."[6] It would be the home of plays like *Ghosts* and *The Ghost Sonata*, *Man and Superman* and *The Doctor's Dilemma*, *Spring's Awakening* and *Lysistrata*.

In the autumn of 1910, Reinhardt tasted the exhilarating directorial experience of arena production when he presented *Oedipus Rex* in the Munich Musikfesthalle, the Circus Renz in Vienna and the Circus Schumann in Berlin. As a result of his success in these and other great arenas, he bought the Circus Schumann as a people's theatre, and conceived the idea for his "Theatre of the Five Thousand." The dream was for a playhouse on the scale of classical Greek and Roman theatres, a theatre for spectacle and ritual designed for large numbers of spectators, the idea of a mass audience carrying a political overtone that impressed a more ideologically committed director like Reinhardt's contemporary, Erwin Piscator. However, Reinhardt's son Gottfried dared to ask of Piscator and of Bertolt Brecht, "Whenever did they perform for the working class as Reinhardt did?"[7]

The spectator in such a theatre was to feel himself to be a participant, a member of a communal event. And to the end, even in California, Reinhardt was still dreaming of a national theatre.[8] Arthur Kahane, his literary adviser, explained the concept as the natural response of the theatre to its times, its "mysterious" link with its age, its desire to create a new and intense relationship between the spectator and the work of art. The secret to success lay in "simplicity":

The vast space demands the simplest of forms, and strong, big, severe lines. All accessories are superfluous; they cannot possibly be noticed, or, if they are, they are a source of distraction. At the most, scenic decoration can only be frame, not function. The elaboration of details, the emphasizing of nuances disappears; the actor and the actor's voice are truly essential, while lighting becomes the real source of decoration, its single aim to bring the important into the light, and to leave the unimportant in the shadow . . . All that is small and petty disappears, and it becomes a matter of course to appeal to the hearts of great audiences with the strongest and deepest elements.[9]

It was a worthy gamble, if an expensive one. The visionary architect Hans Poelzig designed the Grosses Schauspielhaus on the site of the Circus Schumann, and it opened in 1919. It was a vast domed arena seating 3,000, and for the performers a giant thrust stage swept out, embracing a great revolve. There were no curtains separating the actors from their audience, so that the spectator was "gradually

24   The Grosses Schauspielhaus, Berlin, 1919. Architect Hans Poelzig.

to become part of the whole, rapidly absorbed in the action, a member of the chorus, so to speak."[10] Behind the stage rose a permanent cyclorama lit by the Adolf Linnebach system of projected colour and scenery. Kenneth Macgowan thought that "light was the main form of decoration; it emphasized the important and hid the inessential,"[11] and in this he was echoing Kahane, but he was otherwise sceptical about the design. The place had "all the mechanical folderols of the day . . . a great dome, cloud-machine, revolving stage." The lights in the dome made "the first mistake of trying to hide themselves, and the second mistake of not succeeding in doing so." As for the décor, Poelzig had "stained the walls of the many corridors in a yawping red, and turned the main foyer into a ghostly sea-green cavern." This stage was "a gigantic toy," and the theatre itself was "nervous, horrific, clangorous, glowering."[12]

It was eminently suitable for drama on a "heroic" scale. Kahane again: "Though separated by great distances, men still face each other . . . strength and passion become the predominating qualities, the quintessence of tragedy."[13] The kind of production Reinhardt made of the *Oresteia*, the play with which the Grosses Schauspielhaus opened, Rolland's *Danton* and Schiller's *The Robbers* in the years between 1919 and 1921 fully justified the use of so big a stage. Later productions of Offenbach's operettas *Orpheus in the Underworld* and *Tales of Hoffmann* were very much at home. And it is interesting that he was also able to expand and stage *Lysistrata* there, the play which had worked well on the small stage of the Kammerspiele.

Nevertheless, the decision to play Hasenclever's *Antigone* in 1920, as well as the Shakespeare series, *Hamlet, Julius Caesar, The Merchant of Venice* and *A Midsummer Night's Dream*, was questionable. While any of these plays contains a scene or two which can be blown up to the scale of spectacle – the court scenes in *Hamlet*, the forum scene in *Julius Caesar*, the trial scene in *The Merchant of Venice*, for example – the key to a Shakespeare play remains doggedly the intimate relationship between a few characters and between the players and their audience. E. J. Dent felt that the Grosses Schauspielhaus was good for crowd scenes and not much more: "The resonance of the building magnifies every cough or shuffle into a roar, and the only way the actors can make themselves heard is to bawl louder."[14]

And unfortunately, the public for whom this people's theatre was conceived did not always come. Some critics believed that the failure of the Grosses Schauspielhaus, whether as an instrument for communal theatre or for the promotion of dramatic art, was the reason for Reinhardt's giving up control of his theatres in Berlin and moving to Vienna. However that may be, artistic or financial failure did not dampen his enthusiasm for new theatre forms, and he did not abandon the idea of a mass audience. The Salzburg Festival production of *Everyman* in the cathedral square filled him with new ideas, and his move to the beautiful Habsburg city of Vienna, a traditional patron of the arts and the home of great baroque theatres, was an opportunity to experiment yet again.

Reinhardt's association with Vienna after 1920 resulted in the opening of two exquisite theatres in every way different from the Theatre of the Five Thousand. The first was the Theater in der Redoutensaal, the grand ballroom in the Imperial Palace. It was a place of breathtaking beauty, done in the rococo style, scintillating with crystal. Macgowan described the row of Gobelin tapestries hung along the lower walls, and the "mouldings and pilasters, cornices and pargeting, spandrels and pediments, fillets and panelling, an ordered richness of ornament that held suspended in its gray and golden haze mirrors that echoed beauty, and chandeliers radiant with light."[15] Into this wonderfully artificial setting Reinhardt placed his

25   Artist's impression of the Theater in der Redoutensaal, Vienna, 1922.

theatre: a simple stage at one end of the room, done in cream and gold, its design following the lines of the walls, and having no ceiling, no proscenium arch and no wings, borders or backdrops. Above all, there was not even an impression of scenery, only a door on each side and a central curving stairway like an arch arranged to frame an entrance in the middle.

By coincidence, the idea behind the Theater in der Redoutensaal echoed that of Copeau's Vieux Colombier of 1920, a more famous open stage without a proscenium. In both theatres, the audience was to feel itself in the same room with the actors, not merely looking through a frame. The Redoutensaal lacked the gallery running behind the stage of the Vieux Colombier, which was able to compose its actors in the vertical to greater effect. But both shared the same idea of an architectural stage consisting of a bare playing space intended to serve the kind of drama which made little pretence at realism. The emptiness of the stage, and its quality of space and spaciousness, placed a special weight upon the actors: in this theatre "actors must be actors," and the elements of speech, movement and gesture, and of style and stylization in the playing, were made to count. Drama was returned to its fundamentals, and Reinhardt had hit on the perfect vehicle for the delicate domestic and social drama of Goethe's *Clavigo* and *Stella*, and the light-hearted comedy of Calderón's *La dama duende* (*The Fairy Lady*). Reinhardt could not stay in the Redoutensaal, and worked there for only one short season in 1922. However, refusing to give up in Vienna, he turned in 1924 to the Theater in der Josefstadt, a playhouse of great beauty in the best Viennese baroque tradition. There he continued to revive his favourite authors – Shakespeare, Goethe, Schiller, Shaw – until he left Europe in 1934.

The last accomplishment of Reinhardt's career was his development of the open-air production. The organization of an immense dramatic festival came easily to him, and his work on *Everyman* at Salzburg after 1920 moved him to experiment with spatial effects never attempted before. It seemed that his dream of integrating the play and the people finally began to come true. He realized that a permanent festival theatre under cover was necessary to ensure the permanence of the festival itself, and the Salzburg Festspielhaus seating 2,000 was opened in 1925, but he never ceased to hear the call of the outdoor theatre. While *Everyman* continued annually in the Domplatz, in 1931 he offered a sparkling *Twelfth Night* in the garden of his castle home, Leopoldskron, just outside the city, for an invited audience of 250, and made good use of the adjacent lake as the mythical sea-coast of Illyria upon which Viola and Sebastian are stranded. In 1933 he leapt at the chance to try his production of *A Midsummer Night's Dream* in the Boboli Gardens of Florence, and again in the fields outside Oxford. In 1934 and 1935 he tried a spectacular *Merchant of Venice* against a native Italian background, performing it across a real canal in Venice. When in 1934 he found himself in the clement climate of California, he was soon producing *The Dream* against the skies of the Hollywood Bowl and the Faculty Glade of the University of California at Berkeley.

Reinhardt's lasting interest in determining the physical limits of theatrical presentation, its possible range and the factors which controlled the effectiveness of the playing and the response of an audience, was very much at the centre of the theatrical revolution that belongs to the twentieth century. Heinz Herald's well-known assertion, "What, at the Kammerspiele, is a mere relaxation of the fingers, must become a motion of the hand at the Deutsches Theater and a lifting of the arm in the Grosses Schauspielhaus,"[16] may seem obvious to us now, but the profound implications of the statement for the art of drama awaited the proof that Reinhardt supplied by hard practice.

Reinhardt's name is closely linked with the technical development of the theatre in the twentieth century. As the arts and crafts of the stage grew rapidly in proportion to the use of electricity in the early years, so he seized upon every new idea. It was chiefly his work that made the German theatre a byword for advanced technical production, as the reports of ambitious designers and directors like Robert Edmond Jones and Kenneth Macgowan testify.

A revolve (*Drehbühne*, or turntable stage) was first used by Karl Lautenschläger in Munich in 1896, although the Japanese had used turntables as early as the eighteenth century. As many as five or six sets could be erected on the revolve simultaneously, and then each could be moved into view of the audience as needed. Reinhardt readily adopted this device in his Berlin theatres, and it enabled him to change scenes quickly and to present a continuous sequence of action without forgoing too much of the detail of the traditional settings. Thus, a characteristically Elizabethan rhythm of action was brought to the performance of Shakespeare. It was such a convenience that there was some danger that director and designer might use it too often. Supplemented later by other devices of hydraulic machinery designed to move parts of the stage floor and shift scenic units, the revolve completed two centuries of development towards a wholly functional stage.

26 Constructing a set for a revolving stage: four sketches by Ernst Stern. In the last drawing we see through the proscenium frame.

Der komplizierte Beleuchtungsapparat tritt in Tätigkeit.

At the same time, the use of electricity accelerated the change from painted scenery to a more unrealistic, impressionistic setting of colour and light. Paint had thrived in the dim light of the candelabra or the gaslamp, but electricity was infinitely flexible: a switch could change a scene from one tone to another, or plunge it into darkness. As lighting accessories grew more complicated and the ideas of the Swiss lighting designer Adolphe Appia spread, Reinhardt introduced the electric keyboard or "console," the word appropriately borrowed from the bank of keys which played a pipe organ. The operator could "play" the lighting console as if it were a musical instrument, and from the rear of the auditorium one person could control several batteries of lanterns simultaneously, as well as project clouds, stars and a variety of other scenic images.

Reinhardt's development of lighting design went along with the use of the plaster cyclorama at the back of the stage, and of the Mariano Fortuny system of soft, reflected light thrown upon it. The *Rundhorizont,* or curved cyclorama, had been invented in the nineteenth century as a background for a changing panorama; Reinhardt developed the *Kuppelhorizont,* or sky-dome, a hooded cyclorama lit by an *Oberlicht,* a wide floodlight of diffused light designed to increase the illusion of space and infinite depth. To assist this effect, old methods of front lighting by footlights were dispensed with, except for interior scenes. To counterbalance the overhead lights, front-of-house spotlights were installed, and the stage could then be divided into distinctive acting areas, not by scenery or curtains, but by light itself. Light could grant an architectural scene a more convincing, three-dimensional perspective, and the arches and columns, steps and platforms, and other geometrical shapes designed, for example, by Alfred Roller for the Greek plays and for *Faust* gained in their suggestion of an unlocalized, abstract scene.

This emphasis on the technical side of production may suggest that Reinhardt's stage was cluttered and gimmicky. In fact, it could be as stark and simple and as flexible as music, suiting whatever his conception of a play demanded. His inclination was, indeed, away from the fussily realistic scenery of the previous century, and towards the bare stage of the Elizabethan playhouse or the Japanese *kabuki* theatre. His stage had to be as flexible as his wide selection of period styles required. Above all, it had to be efficient, and it was Reinhardt's efficiency as a stage manager that enabled him to undertake such complicated productions as *The Miracle* and *Everyman.* It was this same efficiency that caused Europe and America to speak of "the Reinhardt machine." Yet it was equally characteristic of him to set up a simple arrangement of spotlights directed on a single black curtain at the Kammerspiele, or to pick out a solitary figure in the great space of the Grosses Schauspielhaus. For his abiding principle was to keep the actor at the heart of the play.

Worth special recognition is Reinhardt's encouragement of true repertory. Following a visit to Berlin in 1910, Granville-Barker was critical of the German acting, but he saw that the kind of repertory system that Reinhardt had organized in the Deutsches Theater and the Kammerspiele was unique. He wrote to *The Times* that the organization of two complementary stages gave "in one week a greater variety of good drama than any two London theatres will give in a year."[17]

The concept of repertory is today understood and practised quite widely, to the great advantage of all parties to the play. In the nineteenth century, an age of comparatively inexpensive theatre and short runs, a new play that was unsuccessful at the box-office could be dropped after a night or two. As costs mounted, risks were harder to take, and new plays and new playwrights were particularly handicapped – their playgoing supporters too. Some system which enabled managers to balance profit and loss in any season had to be devised for theatres with some aspiration to producing more demanding works. Ben Iden Payne, who first conceived the British repertory principle when he worked for Miss Annie Horniman at the Dublin Abbey Theatre in 1903, and then again for the same lady at the Manchester Midland and Gaiety Theatres in 1907 and 1908, has indicated another guiding principle: "The dictionary meaning of the word repertory is that it is a storehouse, and that by acquiring a store of good plays, carefully rehearsed, we should be able to make frequent revivals, thereby avoiding – what I particularly condemned – the evil of presenting the public with productions inadequately prepared."[18] But many other virtues accrue. Actors are not trained as automata mechanically repeating the same parts, but gain versatility and extend their talents. When a more popular play supports a less successful one, the theatre itself finds a true place in the community by catering to all tastes with a constant variety of plays. So the principal benefits may belong to the writers and playgoers. The virtues of building and sustaining a known audience are familiar to every kind of theatre, and the merit of putting on a new production only when it is ready, and nursing it over a period of time, is seen today in many national companies.

Back in the 1900s, Reinhardt was an example to the world. Not even the Moscow Art Theatre practised true repertory, and it was the continuing pursuit and success of a regular repertory system in Berlin after 1902 that caused Granville-Barker and others to see for themselves. In the early years, productions like those of Wilde's *Salomé*, Wedekind's *Earth Spirit*, Gorky's *The Lower Depths* and Hofmannsthal's *Electra*, none of them to be classed as popular entertainment, were still running two or three years after the first presentation. Reinhardt maintained a policy of not allowing a production to die if he saw any merit in keeping it alive. The cast might change, but the play was always rehearsed again and a production was always to be improved. As we have seen, major productions like *A Midsummer Night's Dream*, *The Merchant of Venice*, *Faust* and *Oedipus Rex* might survive for decades. A core of actors was engaged by the season, but they usually stayed on for years, and the Reinhardt machine, with the help of assistant directors and two or three *Dramaturgen*, or literary advisers, often had three theatres working simultaneously, supplemented by travelling companies in other cities in Europe and America.

The essential basis for the efficiency of the Reinhardt machine was his method of rehearsal and his development of the *Regiebuch*. His literary advisers Arthur Kahane and Heinz Herald have left accounts of how he prepared a production, and on the evidence of the typical *Regiebuch* have suggested that Reinhardt worked out all the details of a new production in his head long before rehearsals began. He would work alone, perhaps leaving Berlin, in order to be free from the day-to-day work of the office. Once on his own, he would think of nothing else but the play in hand: his favourite hours for such work were apparently between midnight and six or eight in the morning.

At this time he would begin work on the *Regiebuch*, a copy of the play interleaved with blank pages. It was a workshop in itself. Prepared in extraordinary detail, and corrected and modified over and over again, it became the indispensable blueprint from which many assistants could conduct rehearsals while the master watched over the results. In it he would write down every movement and gesture, every expression and tone of voice. Diagrams of the stage plan and even three-dimensional sketches of the scene and its characters would be squeezed into available spaces. Over the years a production lasted, he never finished adding notes in this book, often with pencils and inks of different colours: the *Macbeth* of 1916 is marked in black ink, red ink, red pencil, blue pencil, green pencil and lead pencil, and the

27　A page from the *Macbeth Regiebuch* of 1916, showing plans and a sketch for act II.

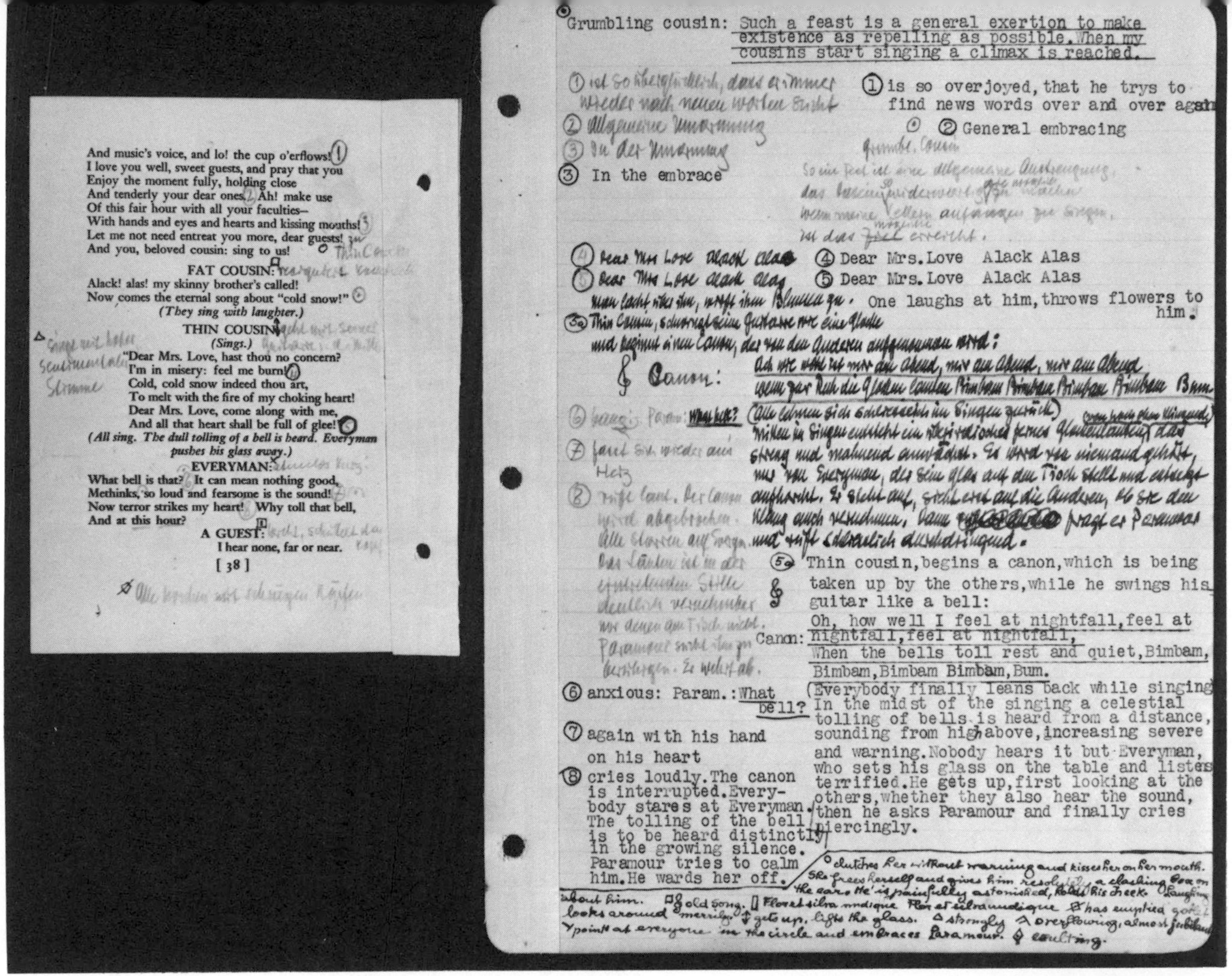

Left page (typescript):

And music's voice, and lo! the cup o'erflows!
I love you well, sweet guests, and pray that you
Enjoy the moment fully, holding close
And tenderly your dear ones. Ah! make use
Of this fair hour with all your faculties—
With hands and eyes and hearts and kissing mouths!
Let me not need entreat you more, dear guest,
And you, beloved cousin: sing to us!

FAT COUSIN:
Alack! alas! my skinny brother's called!
Now comes the eternal song about "cold snow!"
(They sing with laughter.)
THIN COUSIN
"Dear Mrs. Love, hast thou no concern?
I'm in misery: feel me burn!
Cold, cold snow indeed thou art,
To melt with the fire of my choking heart!
Dear Mrs. Love, come along with me,
And all that heart shall be full of glee!"
(All sing. The dull tolling of a bell is heard. Everyman
pushes his glass away.)
EVERYMAN:
What bell is that? It can mean nothing good,
Methinks, 'so loud and fearsome is the sound!
Now terror strikes my heart. Why toll that bell,
And at this hour?
A GUEST:
I hear none, far or near.

[38]

Right page (typescript with handwritten annotations):

Grumbling cousin: Such a feast is a general exertion to make
existence as repelling as possible. Then my
cousins start singing a climax is reached.

① is so overjoyed, that he trys to
find news words over and over again

② General embracing

③ In the embrace

④ Dear Mrs. Love Alack Alas

⑤ Dear Mrs. Love Alack Alas

⑤ One laughs at him, throws flowers to
him.

Canon:

⑤ Thin cousin, begins a canon, which is being
taken up by the others, while he swings his
guitar like a bell:
Oh, how well I feel at nightfall, feel at
Nightfall, feel at nightfall,
Then the bells toll rest and quiet, Bimbam,
Bimbam, Bimbam Bimbam, Bum.

anxious: Param.: What
bell?

⑦ again with his hand
on his heart

⑧ cries loudly. The canon
is interrupted. Every-
body stares at Everyman.
The tolling of the bell
is to be heard distinctly.
Paramour tries to calm
him. He wards her off.

Everybody finally leans back while singing.
In the midst of the singing a celestial
tolling of bells is heard from a distance,
sounding from high above, increasing severe
and warning. Nobody hears it but Everyman,
who sets his glass on the table and listens
terrified. He gets up, first looking at the
others, whether they also hear the sound,
then he asks Paramour and finally cries
piercingly.

28 Pages from the *Everyman Regiebuch* of 1940, when the production was in English in Hollywood

markings appear on the printed page as well as on the blank page, over and under the lines and spilling into the margins.

Each *Regiebuch* is a treasury of ideas and suggestions about the production, about five times the length of the play itself. "When this book is finished," wrote Kahane, "the first picture of the entire work stands ready before his eyes."[19] It reminded Herald of "a closely-woven rug," a complete work with no gaps:

Everything has been taken into consideration, from the most important feature to the least: the atmosphere of every scene, of every conversation in that scene, of every sentence in that conversation. Expression, intonation, every position of the actor, every emotion, the indication of every interval, the effect on the other actors – all these details are mapped out in clear, concise words. At the beginning of each scene, there is a minute description of all the decorations, generally accompanied by drawings, together with a sketch of the stage with full explanations; there is an accurate description of the costume for every new actor, all the crossings within a scene are not only mentioned, but also sketched; the lighting and all the changes in the illumination are described; there are notes on the significance, expression, length, and volume of the music; notes on the different noises; and notes on the way in which the change of scenes is to proceed.[20]

There followed innumerable conferences with the designer and the stage manager, and the physical problems of staging the play were ironed out with more diagrams and sketches. These were then developed into models of the set, and tested in miniature for their possible arrangement on the revolve. The task was like that of fitting together the pieces of a three-dimensional jigsaw puzzle. At this stage the music was also discussed and chosen, because through music Reinhardt could best convey the spirit and atmosphere of the scene he was bringing to life.

Only then did casting begin, an act of infinite care and sensitivity. One of Reinhardt's first decisions upon taking over the Deutsches Theater in 1905 was to open a school of acting, a nursery for his players. A school of acting was also one of his last creations when in 1938 he founded the Max Reinhardt Workshop for Stage, Screen and Radio in Hollywood. At all times in his career he kept the actor at the centre of his attention, and at the same time discouraged the star system he thought damaging to the development of good theatre. He moved his leading actors from one part to another, with understudies stepping into major roles. His casting was always changing, and his concern was always for the whole production. With each actor so well aware of the work of his fellows, the system also encouraged the ensemble work that distinguished all his productions.

Nevertheless, in the matter of casting, Reinhardt was no dictator, and parts were not distributed without a mutual exchange of views on the demands of a role and the powers of the actor. In his story of the New York production of *The Miracle,* Norman Bel Geddes described Reinhardt's way with his players:

Whether the actor was third-rate or famous, Reinhardt began by telling him that he would welcome the actor's interpretation of the part and adapt himself to it. The actor immediately began creating instead of imitating. When the actor's effort was unsuccessful, Reinhardt had a few words with him and the actor became receptive through an awareness of his own limitations. Reinhardt was endlessly patient.[21]

So each actor was encouraged to modify his work, as well as to adjust it to the rest of the ensemble. As the play came alive from that time on, and as everyone made his individual contribution, the original plans accordingly suffered a process of modification.

Reinhardt was a shy man, and as a director a man of few words. He preferred to listen and watch and follow Goethe's advice, "Bilde, Künstler! Rede nicht!" ("Create, artist! Don't speak!"). But all the actors who passed through his hands testified to his strength and commitment as an artist, and to their personal debt to him. Richard Vallentin, who played Satin in *The Lower Depths,* considered that Reinhardt could awaken in his actors things they themselves had never dreamed of.[22] He knew instinctively how far to push them, when to apply a quiet word of praise. He would often act out the lines himself by way of demonstration, and when Glen Byam Shaw made his entrance as the Cripple in *The Miracle,* Reinhardt did not wish him luck, but spat at him to put him in the right frame of mind.[23] He usually went over a part with the actor in private, as the actress Gerda Redlich explained in an interview:

Reinhardt was a very modest, quiet, gentle person. What was typical of him was that when he would sit, he would always sit on his hands, watching what was going on. He would never raise his voice. He did most of his directing by taking actors aside and telling them privately what he wanted to get from them, not in front of the others. It was all gentle and civilized and no showing off at all, just marvellous.[24]

Stella Adler reported that on opening night he would give each player a little bag of sweets, and she added, "It made you feel somebody loved you."[25] Needless to say, he was loved in return.

Rehearsals proper consisted of intense and exact performance, each one demanding more. Reinhardt never tired, and rehearsals stretched into the early hours of the morning. When Francis Lederer played Romeo to Elisabeth Bergner's Juliet in 1928, the dress rehearsal began at 10 a.m. and ended at 2.30 a.m., over sixteen hours. A cut or an addition, a new idea, another detail would be introduced right up to the last minute, and changes would be made even after the play had been running for some time. So it was to the end of his life: on every one of the twelve nights before they closed *Sons and Soldiers,* his disastrous last production, he was in the theatre after the fall of the curtain still polishing the play.[26] One of the reasons why he was never quite happy with film-making was that the growth of his production had to come to an abrupt end when the film was printed.

If there was a characteristic style of Reinhardt acting, it was that of being a little larger than life – more theatrical than the flatter tones of the realists would have allowed, but avoiding the heavy style of the German nineteenth-century theatre. The Reinhardt style knew nothing of the Stanislavsky System or the American Method, but was always vivid and colourful, played essentially to ensure that no important perception would be missed. It was designed to bring audiences into the theatre and not to drive them away.

When Reinhardt rehearsed a crowd scene, his method was necessarily less democratic. Washburn-Freund compared him in this with the conductor of an orchestra: when he directed a "chorus" scene, *"his* will penetrates all these players, *his* feeling pulses through them all, with *his* voice they all shout."[27] Nevertheless, in fundamental ways his method with a crowd of actors was the same as for one. He aimed to inspire enthusiasm for the production as a whole, and never permitted the work to seem perfunctory or impersonal. Each super was encouraged to think both as a member of the group and as an individual. However, in the end it was Reinhardt who orchestrated his players and, with the precision of a chorus in opera, he would arrange his "voices" musically: "A voice starts at one point, is followed by another in an opposite direction, and this in turn is followed by others, and so the cackle spreads like an infection."[28] An emotion like joy or horror would seem first to ripple through the crowd before it burst upon the audience like a shock wave. Gottfried Reinhardt has a glittering passage in which he lists several crowd patterns of his father's choral direction: "These crescendi of mass ecstasy, these huddling diminuendi, the ritardandi of dawning, slowly paralyzing horror, the breathlessly expectant accelerandi, the catatonic rests and vivaciously surging alla-breve passages, the muted fade-outs of predestined doom were symphonic. But Reinhardt was not only the conductor of this unwritten symphony. He was its composer."[29]

Even so, no two crowds were alike in Reinhardt's productions. His assistant Bertold Held wrote in 1919 of the variety of his *Massenregie*

29   Max Reinhardt rehearsing Wilder's *The Merchant of Yonkers* in Boston in 1938.

("crowd control"). For the suffering people of Thebes in Sophocles' *Oedipus Rex* he aimed at "a unity of voice and movement, with several hundred arms stretching up together and a cry from several hundred throats." For the hungry citizens in Hebbel's *Judith* he found the answer by "matching the grief of the individual with the mutual grief of the group, making it more personal." For the revolutionary mob crying out for bread in Büchner's *Danton's Death* he mixed both kinds.[30]

With his giant productions Reinhardt was compelled to adopt almost military tactics. The New York *Miracle* was rehearsed for seven weeks with the help of twenty-two assistants, and in the last two weeks he directed them from a scaffold set up in the middle of the auditorium. Aides stood beside him with megaphones and others were stationed about the house. The *New York Times* correspondent wrote,

From his high post the director controlled and co-ordinated all the elements which entered into the composition of his spectacle. The movable scenery, the light from a hundred points in the house, the organ in one gallery, the choir in the cloisters, the orchestra in another gallery, the bells, the great drums, the wind and thunder machines beneath the stage, the multitude of actors making entrances and exits all over the house, the principals on the stage – all had to be reached.[31]

Reinhardt stood on high, quietly giving orders as he surveyed the field of battle like a general of old.

At times in rehearsal he would be transfigured, and an inspirational fervour would then surge through the whole company. Geddes believed that "his every word and move were nicely calculated to bring the cast to a peak of intensity and performance for the opening curtain."[32] And all this careful persuasion and preparation was more than a matter of assembling a mass of detail, as it had been with the Meiningen company and the theatre of Otto Brahm: Reinhardt's was an hypnotic touch, often something magical. Frank Wedekind called him "the unfathomable magician," and to everyone who worked with him his nickname was *"der grosse Magier,"* "the great magician."

Theatre productions

Date	Author	Production	Theatre

(Where more than one play is listed against a theatre the implication is that they were in repertory.)

1900

	Ibsen	*Love's Comedy*	Deutsches Th., Berlin
	Ibsen	*Love's Comedy*	Somossy Th., Budapest
	Annunzio	*La Gioconda*	Somossy Th., Budapest

1901

Oct. 9	Schneider, Wied, Dreyer	One-act plays	"Schall und Rauch," Berlin

1902

Mar. 11	Strindberg	*The Stronger, The Bond*	"Schall und Rauch," Berlin
Apr. 5	Courteline	*Boubouroche*	"Schall und Rauch," Berlin
Jun. 11		Cabaret sketches	Deutsches Volkstheater, Prague
Jun. 17		Cabaret sketches	Somossy Th., Budapest
Aug. 19	Schneider, Wied, Dreyer	One-act plays	Kleines Th., Berlin
Sep. 25	Feld	*His Highness*	Kleines Th., Berlin
Oct. 13	Strindberg	*Intoxication*	Kleines Th., Berlin
	Strindberg	*There Are Crimes and Crimes*	
Oct. 29	Hollaender and Schmidt	*Ackermann*	Kleines Th., Berlin
Nov. 15	Wilde	*Salomé*	Kleines Th., Berlin
	Wilde	*The Importance of Being Earnest*	
Dec. 17	Wedekind	*Earth Spirit*	Kleines Th., Berlin

128

Date	Author	Production	Theatre
1903			
Jan. 23	Gorky	*The Lower Depths*	Kleines Th., Berlin
Feb. 25	Thoma	*The County Railway*	Neues Th., Berlin
Mar. 19	Anzengruber	*Those Who Sign with a Cross*	Neues Th., Berlin
Apr. 3	Maeterlinck	*Pelléas and Mélisande*	Neues Th., Berlin
Apr. 27	Gorky	*The Lower Depths*	Deutsches Landestheater, Prague
Apr. 29	Hollaender and Schmidt	*Ackermann*	Deutsches Landestheater, Prague
Apr. 30		Cabaret sketches	Deutsches Landestheater, Prague
May 16–27	Gorky	*The Lower Depths*	Magyar Szinház, Budapest
	Wilde	*Salomé*	
	Wedekind	*The Tenor*	
	Halbe	*Youth*	
	Méténier	*Idyll of the Family*	
	Neumann-Hoffer	*Colleagues*	
	Feld	*His Highness*	
	Schnitzler	*Intermezzo*	
Aug. 25	Anzengruber	*Double Suicide*	Neues Th., Berlin
Sep. 4	Wilde	*A Woman of No Importance*	Neues Th., Berlin
Sep. 29	Wilde	*Salomé*	Neues Th., Berlin
Sep. 30	Wedekind	*The Tenor*	Neues Th., Berlin
Oct. 16	Becque	*The Crows*	Kleines Th., Berlin
Oct. 30	Hofmannsthal	*Electra*	Kleines Th., Berlin
Nov. 24	Flers and Caillavet	*The Logic of the Heart*	Neues Th., Berlin
Nov. 27	Wedekind	*King Nicholas, or Such Is Life*	Neues Th., Berlin
Dec. 9	Tolstoy	*The Fruits of Enlightenment*	Neues Th., Berlin
Dec. 19	Halbe	*The Stream*	Neues Th., Berlin
Dec. 31	Bahr	*Among Themselves*	Kleines Th., Berlin
1904			
Jan. 14	Lessing	*Minna von Barnhelm*	Neues Th., Berlin
Jan. 16	Paul	*The Comedy of the Double*	Kleines Th., Berlin
Feb. 10	Shaw	*The Man of Destiny*	Neues Th., Berlin
	Maeterlinck	*Sister Beatrice*	

Date	Author	Production	Theatre
Feb. 19	Euripides	*Medea*	Neues Th., Berlin
Feb. 27	Schmidtbonn	*Mother Highroad*	Kleines Th., Berlin
Mar. 3	Shaw	*Candida*	Neues Th., Berlin
Mar. 12	Schlaikjer	*The Pastor's Rieke*	Kleines Th., Berlin
Mar. 19	Paap	*A King's Right*	Neues Th., Berlin
Apr. 6	Reicke	*Martyrs*	Kleines Th., Berlin
Apr. 12	Auernheimer	*Flirtation*	Neues Th., Berlin
Apr. 22	Schiller	*Love and Intrigue*	Neues Th., Berlin
May 10	Strindberg	*Miss Julie*	Kleines Th., Berlin
May 18	Nestroy	*He Wants to Play a Joke*	Neues Th., Berlin
May 22–	Gorky	*The Lower Depths*	Vigszinház, Budapest
Jun. 10	Schiller	*Love and Intrigue*	
	Halbe	*The Stream*	
	Schlaikjer	*The Pastor's Rieke*	
	Schmidtbonn	*Mother Highroad*	
	Lessing	*Minna von Barnhelm*	
	Méténier	*Idyll of the Family*	
	Dreyer	*Love's Dream*	
	Wedekind	*Earth Spirit*	
	Flers and Caillavet	*The Logic of the Heart*	
	Hofmannsthal	*Electra*	
	Strindberg	*Miss Julie*	
Sep. 23	Wedekind	*Earth Spirit*	Neues Th., Berlin
Oct. 7	Ibsen	*The Pretenders*	Neues Th., Berlin
Oct. 21	Shakespeare	*The Merry Wives of Windsor*	Neues Th., Berlin
Nov. 15	Ruederer	*The Dawn*	Neues Th., Berlin
Nov. 22	Schnitzler	*The Green Cockatoo*	Kleines Th., Berlin
	Schnitzler	*Gallant Cassian*	
Dec. 8	Lange	*The Quiet Rooms*	Kleines Th., Berlin
Dec. 23	Beer-Hofmann	*The Count of Charolais*	Neues Th., Berlin
Dec. 30	Björnson	*The Newly Married Couple*	Kleines Th., Berlin
Dec. 31	Schnitzler	*A Farewell Supper*	Kleines Th., Berlin

1905

Date	Author	Production	Theatre
Jan. 31	Shakespeare	*A Midsummer Night's Dream*	Neues Th., Berlin
Feb. 4	Hartleben	*Angela*	Kleines Th., Berlin
	Hartleben	*Leaving the Regiment*	
Feb. 12	Chekhov	*The Bear*	Kleines Th., Berlin
Mar. 10	Bahr	*Sanna*	Kleines Th., Berlin

Date	Author	Production	Theatre
Mar. 31	Stehr	*Meta Konegen*	Neues Th., Berlin
Apr. 7	Strecker	*Father Riekemann*	Kleines Th., Berlin
Apr. 28	Ibsen	*Rosmersholm*	Kleines Th., Berlin
Oct. 19	Kleist	*Käthchen von Heil-bronn*	Deutsches Th., Berlin
Oct. 22	Lessing	*Minna von Barnhelm*	Deutsches Th., Berlin
Nov. 9	Shakespeare	*The Merchant of Ven-ice*	Deutsches Th., Berlin
Dec. 30	Donnay	*Lovers*	Neues Th., Berlin

1906

Date	Author	Production	Theatre
Jan. 12	Wilde	*A Florentine Tragedy*	Deutsches Th., Berlin
	Synge	*The Well of the Saints*	
	Courteline	*The Commissioner*	
Feb. 2	Hofmannsthal	*Oedipus and the Sphinx*	Deutsches Th., Berlin
Mar. 16	Courteline	*Boubouroche*	Neues Th., Berlin
Mar. 31	Shaw	*Caesar and Cleopatra*	Neues Th., Berlin
Apr. 16	Shakespeare	*A Midsummer Night's Dream*	Neues Deutsches Th., Prague
Apr. 17	Shakespeare	*The Merchant of Ven-ice*	Neues Deutsches Th., Prague
Apr. 25	Molière	*Tartuffe*	Deutsches Th., Berlin
	Goethe	*The Accomplices*	
May 11	Offenbach	*Orpheus in the Underworld*	Neues Th., Berlin
Sep. 15	Shakespeare	*The Winter's Tale*	Deutsches Th., Berlin
Oct. 17	Greiner	*The Love King*	Deutsches Th., Berlin
Nov. 8	Ibsen	*Ghosts*	Kammerspiele, Berlin
Nov. 20	Wedekind	*Spring's Awakening*	Kammerspiele, Berlin
Dec. 6	Shaw	*Man and Superman*	Kammerspiele, Berlin
Dec. 20	Bahr	*The Merry-Go-Round*	Deutsches Th., Berlin

1907

Date	Author	Production	Theatre
Jan. 4	Goethe	*Brothers and Sisters*	Deutsches Th., Berlin
Jan. 7	Hauptmann	*The Feast of Reconcil-iation*	Kammerspiele, Berlin
Jan. 29	Shakespeare	*Romeo and Juliet*	Deutsches Th., Berlin
Mar. 8	Gogol	*The Inspector General*	Deutsches Th., Berlin
Mar. 11	Ibsen	*Hedda Gabler*	Kammerspiele, Berlin
Mar. 19	Asch	*The God of Vengeance*	Deutsches Th., Berlin
Mar. 25	Ibsen	*Love's Comedy*	Kammerspiele, Berlin

Date	Author	Production	Theatre
Apr. 15	Maeterlinck	*Aglavaine and Sély-sette*	Kammerspiele, Berlin
Apr. 25	Raeder	*Robert and Bertram*	Deutsches Th., Berlin
May 2	Hebbel	*Gyges and His Ring*	Kammerspiele, Berlin
May 6–15	Asch	*The God of Vengeance*	Vigszinház, Budapest
	Hauptmann	*The Feast of Reconcil-iation*	
	Wilde	*The Importance of Being Earnest*	
	Hartleben	*Angela*	
	Courteline	*The Commissioner*	
	Wedekind	*Spring's Awakening*	
	Wedekind	*The Tenor*	
	Strindberg	*The Dance of Death*	
Aug. 29	Strindberg	*Miss Julie*	Kammerspiele, Berlin
Sep. 14	Kleist	*The Prince of Homburg*	Deutsches Th., Berlin
Sep. 19	Schnitzler	*Light o' Love*	Kammerspiele, Berlin
Oct. 17	Shakespeare	*Twelfth Night*	Deutsches Th., Berlin
Oct. 26	Grillparzer	*Esther*	Kammerspiele, Berlin
	Goldoni	*The Servant of Two Masters*	
Nov. 9	Wedekind	*The Marquis of Keith*	Kammerspiele, Berlin
	Shakespeare	*A Midsummer Night's Dream*	Deutsches Th., Berlin
Dec. 9	Vollmoeller	*Catherine, Countess of Armagnac and Her Two Lovers*	Kammerspiele, Berlin
Dec. 20	Calderón	*The Doctor on His Honour*	Deutsches Th., Berlin

1908

Date	Author	Production	Theatre
Jan. 10	Schiller	*The Robbers*	Deutsches Th., Berlin
Jan. 23	Strauss	*Wedding*	Kammerspiele, Berlin
Feb. 27	Aristophanes	*Lysistrata*	Kammerspiele, Berlin
Mar. 7	L'Arronge	*The Partner*	Deutsches Th., Berlin
Mar. 30	Hofmannsthal	*Death and the Fool*	Kammerspiele, Berlin
	Dymow	*Nju*	
May 16	Eulenberg	*Ulrich, Prince of Wal-deck*	Deutsches Th., Berlin
May 22–	Shakespeare	*The Merchant of Ven-ice*	Vigszinház, Budapest
Jun. 4	Shakespeare	*A Midsummer Night's Dream*	
	Gogol	*The Inspector General*	
	L'Arronge	*The Partner*	
	Heijermans	*Links*	

Date	Author	Production	Theatre
	Schnitzler	*Light o' Love*	
	Schiller	*The Robbers*	
	Wedekind	*Spring's Awakening*	
	Wilde	*Salomé*	
	Dymow	*Nju*	
Aug. 8	Grillparzer	*The Waves of the Ocean and of Love*	Deutsches Th., Berlin
Aug. 25	Grillparzer	*Medea*	Deutsches Th., Berlin
Sep. 4	Holz	*Social Aristocrats*	Kammerspiele, Berlin
Sep. 9	Heijermans	*Links*	Deutsches Th., Berlin
Sep. 14	Izumo Gersdorff	*Terakoya Kimiko*	Kammerspiele, Berlin
Sep. 16	Shakespeare	*King Lear*	Deutsches Th., Berlin
Sep. 29	Schiller	*Love and Intrigue*	Deutsches Th., Berlin
Oct. 16	Goethe	*Clavigo*	Kammerspiele, Berlin
Oct. 21	Schiller	*Fiesco,* or *The Genoese Conspiracy*	Deutsches Th., Berlin
Oct. 30	Gogol	*The Wedding*	Kammerspiele, Berlin
Nov. 14	Nestroy	*Revolution in Kräh- winkel*	Deutsches Th., Berlin
Nov. 21	Shaw	*The Doctor's Dilemma*	Kammerspiele, Berlin
Dec. 5	Wolff	*No One Knows*	Kammerspiele, Berlin
Dec. 22	Schmidtbonn	*The Count of Gleichen*	Kammerspiele, Berlin

1909

Date	Author	Production	Theatre
Jan. 29	Brody	*The Teacher*	Deutsches Th., Berlin
Mar. 25	Goethe	*Faust I*	Deutsches Th., Berlin
Apr. 25	Ruederer	*Wolkenkuckucksheim*	Kammerspiele, Berlin
May 4	Wolzogen	*The Man Who Found No Sympathy*	Kammerspiele, Berlin
May 22–	Shakespeare	*Twelfth Night*	Vigszinház, Budapest
Jun. 4	Shaw	*The Doctor's Dilemma*	
	Nestroy	*Revolution in Kräh- winkel*	
	Aristophanes	*Lysistrata*	
	Schmidtbonn	*The Count of Gleichen*	
	Brody	*The Teacher*	
	Shakespeare	*Hamlet*	
	Wedekind	*Spring's Awakening*	
	Goethe	*Faust I*	
May	Aristophanes	*Lysistrata*	Breslau
	Nestroy	*Revolution in Kräh- winkel*	
Jun.	Shakespeare	*Hamlet*	Künstler Th., Munich
	Shakespeare	*A Midsummer Night's Dream*	

Date	Author	Production	Theatre
	Goethe	*Faust I*	
	Shakespeare	*Twelfth Night*	
	Schiller	*The Robbers*	
Jul.	Schiller	*The Robbers*	Frankfurt-on-Main
	Aristophanes	*Lysistrata*	
	Shakespeare	*Twelfth Night*	
Oct. 8	Nicodemi	*The Refuge*	Kammerspiele, Berlin
Oct. 16	Shakespeare	*Hamlet*	Deutsches Th., Berlin
Nov. 5	Shaw	*Major Barbara*	Kammerspiele, Berlin
Nov. 10	Schiller	*Don Carlos*	Deutsches Th., Berlin
Dec. 9	Mirbeau and Natanson	*The Home*	Kammerspiele, Berlin
Dec. 15	Shakespeare	*The Taming of the Shrew*	Deutsches Th., Berlin

1910

Date	Author	Production	Theatre
Jan. 19	Rivoire and Salten	*Good King Dagobert*	Deutsches Th., Berlin
Jan. 21	Eulenberg	*The Natural Father*	Kammerspiele, Berlin
Feb. 11	Hofmannsthal	*Christina's Homecoming*	Deutsches Th., Berlin
Feb. 25	Hebbel	*Judith*	Deutsches Th., Berlin
Feb. 28	Schmidtbonn	*Help! A Child Has Fallen from Heaven*	Kammerspiele, Berlin
Mar. 30	Stucken	*Gawân*	Kammerspiele, Berlin
Apr. 12	Schiller	*The Bride of Messina*	Deutsches Th., Berlin
Apr. 22	Freksa	*Sumurûn*	Kammerspiele, Berlin
			Deutsches Th., Berlin
May 1–10	Shakespeare	*The Taming of the Shrew*	Vigszinház, Budapest
	Rivoire	*Good King Dagobert*	
	Hebbel	*Judith*	
	Ibsen	*Ghosts*	
	Shakespeare	*The Winter's Tale*	
	Hofmannsthal	*Christina's Homecoming*	
	Stucken	*Gawân*	
May 11–29	Shakespeare	*A Midsummer Night's Dream*	Burgtheater, Vienna
	Lessing	*Minna von Barnhelm*	
	Bahr	*Sanna*	
	Beer-Hofmann	*The Count of Charolais*	
	Hofmannsthal	*Christina's Homecoming*	
	Shakespeare	*The Merchant of Venice*	

Date	Author	Production	Theatre
	Freksa	*Sumurûn*	
	Shakespeare	*Hamlet*	
	Shakespeare	*Twelfth Night*	
	Aristophanes	*Lysistrata*	
	Schiller	*The Robbers*	
	Hebbel	*Judith*	
Spring	Shakespeare	*The Merchant of Venice*	Brussels
Jun.	Shakespeare	*The Merchant of Venice*	Künstler Th., Munich
	Shakespeare	*A Midsummer Night's Dream*	
	Shakespeare	*The Winter's Tale*	
	Shakespeare	*Twelfth Night*	
	Aristophanes	*Lysistrata*	
	Lessing	*Minna von Barnhelm*	
Aug. 19	Lange	*Samson and Delilah*	Deutsches Th., Berlin
Sep. 5	Kleist	*Amphitryon*	Deutsches Th., Berlin
Sep. 6	Gorky	*The Last*	Kammerspiele, Berlin
Sep. 21	Rostand	*The Romantics*	Deutsches Th., Berlin
Sep. 23	Verhaeren	*The Cloister*	Kammerspiele, Berlin
Sep. 25	Sophocles	*Oedipus Rex*	Musikfesthalle, Munich
Oct. 7	Molière	*The Forced Marriage*	Kammerspiele, Berlin
	Shakespeare	*The Comedy of Errors*	
Oct. 10	Sophocles	*Oedipus Rex*	Circus Renz, Vienna
Oct. 29	Fulda	*Master and Servant*	Deutsches Th., Berlin
Nov. 7	Sophocles	*Oedipus Rex*	Circus Schumann, Berlin
Nov. 18	Capus	*The Wounded Bird*	Kammerspiele, Berlin
Nov. 24	Shakespeare	*Hamlet*	Deutsches Th., Berlin
Dec. 8	Capus	*An Angel*	Kammerspiele, Berlin
Dec. 10	Shakespeare	*Othello*	Deutsches Th., Berlin
Dec. 31	Nestroy	*The Jolly Vagabonds*	Deutsches Th., Berlin

1911

Date	Author	Production	Theatre
Jan. 3	Stucken	*Lancelot*	Kammerspiele, Berlin
Jan. 26	Strauss	*Der Rosenkavalier*	Royal Opera House, Dresden
Jan. 30	Freksa	*Sumurûn*	Coliseum, London
			Savoy Theatre, London
Feb. 2	Pinski	*The Treasure*	Deutsches Th., Berlin
Feb. 6	Lessing	*Minna von Barnhelm*	Bellevue Castle, Berlin
Feb. 7	Vollmoeller	*Wieland*	Deutsches Th., Berlin

Date	Author	Production	Theatre
Feb. 15	Sternheim	*The Giant*	Kammerspiele, Berlin
Mar. 15	Goethe	*Faust II*	Deutsches Th., Berlin
Mar. 23	Sophocles	*Oedipus Rex*	Interimtheater, Riga
Mar. 25	Sophocles	*Oedipus Rex*	Circus Ciniselli, St Petersburg
Mar. 29	Wolff	*The Queen*	Kammerspiele, Berlin
Apr. 18	Sophocles	*Oedipus Rex*	Zirkus im Tiergarten, Stockholm
Apr. 21–30	Molière	*The Forced Marriage*	Vigszinház, Budapest
	Shakespeare	*The Comedy of Errors*	
	Freksa	*Sumurûn*	
	Lange	*Samson and Delilah*	
	Sternheim	*Knickers*	
	Capus	*The Wounded Bird*	
	Katona	*The Viceroy*	
Apr. 29	Sophocles	*Oedipus Rex*	Neues Deutsches Th., Prague
May 24	Katona	*The Viceroy*	Deutsches Th., Berlin
May 31	Aeschylus	*Oresteia*	Circus Busch, Berlin
Jun. 14	Aeschylus	*Oresteia*	Leipzig
Jun. 30	Offenbach	*La Belle Hélène*	Künstler Th., Munich
Aug. 26	Freksa	*The Fat Caesar*	Deutsches Th., Berlin
Aug. 31	Aeschylus	*Oresteia*	Musikfesthalle, Munich
Sep. 9	Stucken	*Lanvâl*	Kammerspiele, Berlin
Sep. 16	Sophocles	*Oedipus Rex*	Circus Beketow, Budapest
Sep. 23	Kleist	*Penthesilea*	Deutsches Th., Berlin
Sep. 25	Sophocles	*Oedipus Rex*	Stadttheater, Zurich
Oct. 3	Sophocles	*Oedipus Rex*	Magyar Szinház, Budapest
Oct. 5	Scholz	*Souls Exchanged*	Kammerspiele, Berlin
Oct. 6	Offenbach	*La Belle Hélène*	Th. in der Josefstadt, Vienna
Oct. 9	Lessing	*Nathan the Wise*	Kammerspiele, Berlin
Oct. 10	Sophocles	*Oedipus Rex*	Circus Busch, Berlin
Oct. 13	Aeschylus	*Oresteia*	Circus Schumann, Berlin
Oct. 27	Gozzi	*Turandot*	Deutsches Th., Berlin
Nov. 1	Sophocles	*Oedipus Rex*	Stadttheater, Amsterdam
	Sophocles	*Oedipus Rex*	Royal Th., The Hague
Nov. 24	Sternheim	*The Small Box*	Deutsches Th., Berlin
Dec. 1	Hofmannsthal	*Everyman*	Circus Schumann, Berlin
Dec. 15	Unruh	*Officers*	Deutsches Th., Berlin
Dec. 23	Vollmoeller	*The Miracle*	Olympia, London

Date	Author	Production	Theatre
1912			
Winter	Sophocles	*Oedipus Rex*	St Petersburg, Moscow, Riga, Warsaw, Kiev, Odessa, Stockholm
	Shakespeare	*Hamlet*	Deutsches Th., Berlin
	Shakespeare	*Romeo and Juliet*	Deutsches Th., Berlin
Jan. 13	Schmidtbonn	*The Wrath of Achilles*	Deutsches Th., Berlin
Jan. 15	Sophocles	*Oedipus Rex*	Covent Garden, London
Jan. 16	Freksa	*Sumurûn*	Casino Th., New York
Jan. 20	Nansen	*A Happy Marriage*	Kammerspiele, Berlin
Jan. 23	Shakespeare	*Much Ado About Nothing*	Deutsches Th., Berlin
Mar. 19	Courteline and Wolff	*I'm Fed Up with Margot*	Kammerspiele, Berlin
	Arnold	*Pierrot's Last Adventure*	
Mar. 23	Sophocles	*Oedipus Rex*	Riga
Mar. 26	Heimann	*Enemy and Brother*	Kammerspiele, Berlin
Apr. 3	Sophocles	*Oedipus Rex*	Circus Nikitin, Moscow
Apr. 11	Sophocles	*Oedipus Rex*	Kharkov
Apr. 13	Molière	*George Dandin*	Deutsches Th., Berlin
Apr. 14	Sophocles	*Oedipus Rex*	Odessa
Apr. 16	Sophocles	*Oedipus Rex*	Circus Hippodrome Palace, Kiev
Apr. 21–30	Gozzi	*Turandot*	Vigszinház, Budapest
	Hebbel	*Gyges and His Ring*	
	Hofmannsthal	*Everyman*	
	Nansen	*A Happy Marriage*	
May	Hofmannsthal	*Everyman*	Frankfurt-on-Main
May 7	Rivoire and Besnard	*My Friend Teddy*	Kammerspiele, Berlin
May 12	Hofmannsthal	*Everyman*	Neues Deutsches Th., Prague
May 25	Freksa	*Sumurûn*	Théâtre du Vaudeville, Paris
Jun. 4	Wedekind	*Hidalla*	Deutsches Th., Berlin
June. 7	Wedekind	*Music*	Deutsches Th., Berlin
Jun. 12	Wedekind	*Oaha*	Deutsches Th., Berlin
Jun. 15	Wedekind	*The Marquis of Keith*	Deutsches Th., Berlin
Aug.	Aeschylus	*Oresteia*	Austellungs Halle, Munich
	Offenbach	*Orpheus in the Underworld*	

Date	Author	Production	Theatre
Sep.	Vollmoeller	*The Miracle*	Rotunde Th., Vienna
Sep. 13	Sternheim	*Don Juan*	Deutsches Th., Berlin
Sep. 27	Strindberg	*The Dance of Death*	Deutsches Th., Berlin
Oct. 12	Shakespeare	*Henry IV, Part I*	Deutsches Th., Berlin
Oct. 18	Shakespeare	*Henry IV, Part II*	Deutsches Th., Berlin
Oct.	Vollmoeller	*The Miracle*	Elberfeld, Breslau, Cologne
Oct. 25	Molière	*The Would-Be Gentleman*	Royal Opera House, Stuttgart
	Strauss	*Ariadne auf Naxos*	
Nov. 11	Vollmoeller	*Venetian Night*	Palace Th., London
Nov. 12	Hebbel	*Maria Magdalene*	Kammerspiele, Berlin
Nov. 23	Maeterlinck	*The Blue Bird*	Deutsches Th., Berlin
Winter	Hofmannsthal	*Everyman*	Vigszinház, Budapest
	Gozzi	*Turandot*	
	Hebbel	*Gyges and His Ring*	

1913

Date	Author	Production	Theatre
Jan. 3	Mann	*Fiorenza*	Kammerspiele, Berlin
Jan. 17	Rey	*Beautiful Women*	Kammerspiele, Berlin
Jan. 24	Stucken	*Astrid*	Deutsches Th., Berlin
Jan. 25	Vollmoeller	*The Miracle*	Neues Deutsches Th., Prague
Feb. 7	Tolstoy	*The Living Corpse*	Deutsches Th., Berlin
Feb. 15	Vollmoeller	*The Miracle*	Volksoper, Vienna
Mar. 5	Sternheim	*Citizen Schippel*	Kammerspiele, Berlin
Apr. 4	Guitry	*The Conquest of Berg-op-Zoom*	Kammerspiele, Berlin
May	Tolstoy	*The Living Corpse*	Prague
May 5	Freksa	*Sumurûn*	Coliseum, London
May 8	Asch	*The League of the Weak*	Kammerspiele, Berlin
May 22–Jun. 1	Tolstoy	*The Living Corpse*	Vigszinház, Budapest
	Hofmannsthal	*Everyman*	
	Wedekind	*Spring's Awakening*	
	Asch	*The League of the Weak*	
	Maeterlinck	*The Blue Bird*	
	Strindberg	*The Dance of Death*	
	Wedekind	*Music*	
May 31	Hauptmann	*The Centenary Festival 1813*	Centenary Hall, Breslau
Jun. 4	Mees	*His Imperial Highness*	Kammerspiele, Berlin
Aug. 29	Vollmoeller	*Venetian Night*	Kammerspiele, Berlin
	Strindberg	*The Stronger*	

Date	Author	Production	Theatre
Sep. 5	Wedekind	*Francisca*	Kammerspiele, Berlin
Sep.	Vollmoeller	*The Miracle*	Leipzig
	Vollmoeller	*The Miracle*	Dresden
	Wedekind	*Music*	Dresden
	Ibsen	*Ghosts*	Dresden
Sep. 17	Goethe	*Torquato Tasso*	Deutsches Th., Berlin
Oct. 1	Flers and Cail-lavet	*The Green Coat*	Kammerspiele, Berlin
Oct.	Vollmoeller	*The Miracle*	Elberfeld, Breslau, Cologne, Prague
	Freksa	*Sumurûn*	Théâtre du Vaudeville, Paris
Oct. 24	Schmidtbonn	*The Prodigal Son*	Kammerspiele, Berlin
Oct. 31	Lessing	*Emilia Galotti*	Kammerspiele, Berlin
Nov. 14	Shakespeare	*A Midsummer Night's Dream*	Deutsches Th., Berlin
Nov. 21	Shakespeare	*Much Ado About Nothing*	Deutsches Th., Berlin
Nov. 25	Shaw	*Androcles and the Lion*	Kammerspiele, Berlin
Dec. 1	Shakespeare	*Hamlet*	Deutsches Th., Berlin
Dec. 10	Strindberg	*The Storm*	Kammerspiele, Berlin
Dec. 15	Shakespeare	*The Merchant of Venice*	Deutsches Th., Berlin
Dec. 29	Becque	*La Parisienne*	Kammerspiele, Berlin
Dec.	Vollmoeller	*The Miracle*	Frankfurt-on-Main
Films made in 1913:			
	Vollmoeller	*Venetian Night*	
	Kahane	*The Island of the Blessed*	

1914

Date	Author	Production	Theatre
Jan. 15	Shakespeare	*King Lear*	Deutsches Th., Berlin
Jan. 28	Shakespeare	*Romeo and Juliet*	Deutsches Th., Berlin
Jan.	Vollmoeller	*The Miracle*	Hamburg, Karlsruhe
Feb. 2	Sternheim	*The Snob*	Kammerspiele, Berlin
Feb. 11	Shakespeare	*Henry IV, Part I*	Deutsches Th., Berlin
Feb. 20	Shakespeare	*Henry IV, Part II*	Deutsches Th., Berlin
Mar.	Schmidtbonn	*The Prodigal Son*	Hamburg
Mar. 6	Hamsun	*In the Grip of Life*	Kammerspiele, Berlin
Mar. 13	Shakespeare	*Twelfth Night*	Deutsches Th., Berlin
Mar. 18	Shakespeare	*Othello*	Deutsches Th., Berlin
Mar. 30	Hazelton and Benrimo	*The Yellow Jacket*	Kammerspiele, Berlin
Apr.	Sternheim	*The Snob*	Frankfurt-on-Main
Apr. 14	Strindberg	*The Pelican*	Kammerspiele, Berlin
Apr. 28	Halbe	*Freedom*	Kammerspiele, Berlin

Date	Author	Production	Theatre
Apr.	Strindberg	*The Pelican*	Vienna
Apr. 30	Vollmoeller	*The Miracle*	Circus Busch, Berlin
May	Schmidtbonn	*The Prodigal Son*	Vienna, Prague, Bremen
	Strindberg	*The Pelican*	
	Strindberg	*The Storm*	
	Ibsen	*Ghosts*	
	Sternheim	*Citizen Schippel*	
	Sternheim	*The Snob*	
May 23–30	Strindberg	*The Pelican*	Vigszinház, Budapest
	Schmidtbonn	*The Prodigal Son*	
	Ibsen	*Ghosts*	
	Sternheim	*Citizen Schippel*	
	Strindberg	*The Storm*	
	Sternheim	*The Snob*	
Jun. 9	Wedekind	*The Stone of Wisdom*	Kammerspiele, Berlin
Jun. 11	Hofmannsthal	*Everyman*	Metropol Th., Berlin
Aug. 28	Kleist	*The Prince of Homburg*	Deutsches Th., Berlin
Sep. 12	Gutzkow	*Queue and Sword*	Deutsches Th., Berlin
Sep. 25	Schmidtbonn	*1914*	Deutsches Th., Berlin
	Schiller	*Wallenstein's Camp*	
Oct. 9	Schiller	*The Piccolomini*	Deutsches Th., Berlin
Oct. 30	Kotzebue	*The German Provincials*	Kammerspiele, Berlin
Nov. 13	Schiller	*The Death of Wallenstein*	Deutsches Th., Berlin
Dec. 8	Hebbel	*Genevieve*	Deutsches Th., Berlin
Dec. 30	Shakespeare	*The Winter's Tale*	Deutsches Th., Berlin

1915

Date	Author	Production	Theatre
Jan. 18	Raimund	*Firehead*	Deutsches Th., Berlin
Feb. 26	Sternheim	*The Charming Fellow*	Kammerspiele, Berlin
Mar. 18	Hauptmann	*Schluck and Jau*	Deutsches Th., Berlin
Apr. 6	Schönherr	*The Demon in Woman*	Kammerspiele, Berlin
May 21	Goethe	*The Fair at Plundersweiler*	Deutsches Th., Berlin
Sep. 1	Schiller	*The Robbers*	Volksbühne, Berlin
Sep. 3	Kotzebue	*The German Provincials*	Volksbühne, Berlin
Sep. 13	Hebbel	*Judith*	Deutsches Th., Berlin
Sep. 15	Shakespeare	*The Merchant of Venice*	Volksbühne, Berlin
Sep. 29	Hauptmann	*Colleague Crampton*	Deutsches Th., Berlin
Oct. 8	Shakespeare	*The Tempest*	Volksbühne, Berlin
Oct. 27	Strindberg	*The Father*	Kammerspiele, Berlin

Date	Author	Production	Theatre
Oct. 27	Harlan	*The Egg of Nuremberg*	Deutsches Th., Berlin
Oct. 29	Schiller	*Maria Stuart*	Deutsches Th., Berlin
Nov. 5	Wedekind	*The Love Potion*	Kammerspiele, Berlin
Nov. 9–16	Schiller	*The Robbers*	Royal Opera, Stock-
	Shakespeare	*Twelfth Night*	holm
	Goethe	*Faust I*	
	Lessing	*Minna von Barnhelm*	
	Shakespeare	*A Midsummer Night's Dream*	
	Strindberg	*The Dance of Death*	
	Shakespeare	*Macbeth*	
	Ibsen	*Ghosts*	
	Hauptmann	*The Beaver Coat*	
Nov. 18–20	Strindberg	*The Dance of Death*	National Th., Christiana
	Lessing	*Minna von Barnhelm*	
Nov. 29	Holz and Jerschke	*Traumulus*	Volksbühne, Berlin
Dec. 17	Vollmoeller	*The Miracle*	Volksbühne, Berlin
Dec. 27	Falkenberg	*The Star of Bethlehem*	Deutsches Th., Berlin

1916

Date	Author	Production	Theatre
Jan. 12	Hauptmann	*The Beaver Coat*	Deutsches Th., Berlin
Jan. 25	Shakespeare	*Much Ado About Nothing*	Volksbühne, Berlin
Feb. 5	Sophocles	*Oedipus Rex*	Volksbühne, Berlin
Feb. 18	Hauptmann	*Drayman Henschel*	Volksbühne, Berlin
Feb. 29	Shakespeare	*Macbeth*	Deutsches Th., Berlin
Mar. 10	Molière	*The Imaginary Invalid*	Kammerspiele, Berlin
Mar. 16	Hofmannsthal	*The Shepherdesses*	Kammerspiele, Berlin
Mar. 21	Anzengruber	*Double Suicide*	Volksbühne, Berlin
Apr. 18	Kalisch and Weirauch	*The People of Mottenburg*	Volksbühne, Berlin
Apr. 20	Shakespeare	*Romeo and Juliet*	Volksbühne, Berlin
Apr. 26	Hofmannsthal	*The Bores*	Deutsches Th., Berlin
	Mozart	*The Magic Flute*	
Apr. 28–	Shakespeare	*Macbeth*	Grosses Schauspiel-
May	Strindberg	*The Dance of Death*	haus, Rotterdam; The Hague; Stadttheater, Amsterdam
	Shakespeare	*Twelfth Night*	
	Lessing	*Minna von Barnhelm*	
	Ibsen	*Ghosts*	
	Hauptmann	*The Beaver Coat*	
May 19–21	Hauptmann	*Colleague Crampton*	Vigszinház, Budapest

Date	Author	Production	Theatre
	Strindberg	*The Father*	
	Hauptmann	*Drayman Henschel*	
	Strindberg	*The Dance of Death*	
	Kotzebue	*The German Pro-vincials*	
	Hauptmann	*The Beaver Coat*	
	Lessing	*Minna von Barnhelm*	
Sep. 2	Wedekind	*The Rapid Painter*	Kammerspiele, Berlin
Sep. 9	Hauptmann	*Rose Bernd*	Deutsches Th., Berlin
Sep. 16	Ibsen	*Hedda Gabler*	Kammerspiele, Berlin
Sep. 22	Strindberg	*Master Olof*	Volksbühne, Berlin
Sep. 30	Mitchell	*The New York Idea*	Kammerspiele, Berlin
Oct. 13	Lenz	*Soldiers*	Deutsches Th., Berlin
Oct. 20	Strindberg	*The Ghost Sonata*	Kammerspiele, Berlin
Oct. 30	Klinger and Sternheim	*The Suffering Woman*	Deutsches Th., Berlin
Nov. 9	Lessing	*Minna von Barnhelm*	Deutsches Th., Berlin
Nov. 17	Schiller	*Love and Intrigue*	Deutsches Th., Berlin
Nov. 29	Wildgans	*Poverty and Love*	Kammerspiele, Berlin
Nov.	Mozart	*The Magic Flute*	Hamburg, Dusseldorf, Duisberg, Mann- heim
Dec. 15	Büchner	*Danton's Death*	Deutsches Th., Berlin
Dec. 23	Hauptmann	*The Rats*	Volksbühne, Berlin
Dec. 31	Beaumarchais	*The Marriage of Figaro*	Deutsches Th., Berlin

1917

Date	Author	Production	Theatre
Jan. 4–23	Aeschylus	*Oresteia*	Stadttheater, Zurich; Bern; Basle; St Gal- len; Davos; Lucerne
	Shakespeare	*A Midsummer Night's Dream*	
	Schiller	*Love and Intrigue*	
	Strindberg	*The Dance of Death*	
	Shakespeare	*Twelfth Night*	
	Büchner	*Danton's Death*	
	Hauptmann	*Rose Bernd*	
	Strindberg	*The Ghost Sonata*	
	Kotzebue	*The German Pro-vincials*	
Jan. 30	Bahr	*The Concert*	Kammerspiele, Berlin
Feb. 10	Grillparzer	*Woe to the Liar*	Volksbühne, Berlin
Feb. 15	Shakespeare	*Othello*	Deutsches Th., Berlin
Mar. 8	Hebbel	*Judith*	Deutsches Th., Berlin
Mar. 14	Ibsen	*John Gabriel Borkman*	Deutsches Th., Berlin

Date	Author	Production	Theatre
Mar. 16	Anzengruber	*The Gnawing Conscience*	Volksbühne, Berlin
Mar. 26	Hauptmann (Carl)	*Tobias Buntschuh*	Deutsches Th., Berlin
Apr. 2	Molnár	*Carnival*	Kammerspiele, Berlin
Apr. 16	Molière	*The Miser*	Deutsches Th., Berlin
Apr. 20	Schönherr	*A People in Trouble*	Volksbühne, Berlin
May 11	Hauptmann	*Elga*	Volksbühne, Berlin
May 2–10	Shakespeare	*Othello*	Royal Opera, Stockholm
	Strindberg	*The Ghost Sonata*	
	Gorky	*The Lower Depths*	
	Hauptmann	*Rose Bernd*	
	Kotzebue	*The German Provincials*	
	Lessing	*Minna von Barnhelm*	
	Vollmoeller	*The Miracle*	
May 9–13	Hauptmann	*Rose Bernd*	Lorensbergstheater, Göteborg; Malmö; Helsingborg
	Strindberg	*The Ghost Sonata*	
	Gorky	*The Lower Depths*	
	Lessing	*Minna von Barnhelm*	
	Kotzebue	*The German Provincials*	
Jun.	Hauptmann	*Rose Bernd*	Basle, Bern, Zurich, St Gallen, Schaffhausen, Lucerne, Davos
	Strindberg	*The Ghost Sonata*	
	Büchner	*Danton's Death*	
	Kotzebue	*The German Provincials*	
Jun.	Lessing	*Minna von Barnhelm*	Bucharest
	Schiller	*Love and Intrigue*	
	Shakespeare	*Twelfth Night*	
	Vollmoeller	*The Miracle*	
	Shakespeare	*The Merchant of Venice*	
Sep. 3	Wolzogen	*The Mob*	Volksbühne, Berlin
Sep. 13	Jensen and Vollmoeller	*Madame d'Ora*	Kammerspiele, Berlin
Sep. 25	Tolstoy	*The Living Corpse*	Deutsches Th., Berlin
Oct. 17	Hauptmann	*Winter Ballad*	Deutsches Th., Berlin
Oct. 21	Sophocles	*Oedipus Rex*	Volksbühne, Berlin
Oct. 26	Salten	*The Children of Joy*	Kammerspiele, Berlin
Nov. 19	Gött	*The Deer*	Volksbühne, Berlin

Date	Author	Production	Theatre
Nov. 23	Ibsen	*A Doll's House*	Kammerspiele, Berlin
Dec. 14	Reicke	*Blood Sacrifice*	Volksbühne, Berlin
Dec. 23	Sorge	*The Beggar*	Deutsches Th., Berlin

1918

Date	Author	Production	Theatre
Jan. 17	Kaiser	*The Coral*	Kammerspiele, Berlin
Jan. 25	Kleist	*Hermann's Battle*	Volksbühne, Berlin
Feb. 9	Tolstoy	*The Power of Darkness*	Deutsches Th., Berlin
Feb. 23	Hauptmann	*The Assumption of Hannele*	Volksbühne, Berlin
Feb. 26	Strindberg	*The Black Glove*	Kammerspiele, Berlin
Mar. 3	Goering	*A Sea Battle*	Kammerspiele, Berlin
Mar. 24	Hasenclever	*The Son*	Kammerspiele, Berlin
Apr. 9	Molière	*The Would-Be Gentleman*	Deutsches Th., Berlin
Apr. 13	Fulda	*The Right One*	Volksbühne, Berlin
May 7	Shakespeare	*King Lear*	Volksbühne, Berlin
Jun. 9	Werfel	*The Visitor from Elysium*	Kammerspiele, Berlin
	Koffka	*Cain*	
Sep. 13	Goethe	*Clavigo*	Kleines Schauspielhaus, Berlin
Sep. 18	Schiller	*Maria Stuart*	Deutsches Th., Berlin
Sep. 21	Giedion	*Labour*	Kleines Schauspielhaus, Berlin
Sep. 29	Wedekind	*Spring's Awakening*	Kleines Schauspielhaus, Berlin
Oct. 25	Goering	*The First One*	Kammerspiele, Berlin
Oct. 31	Racine	*Phèdre*	Kleines Schauspielhaus, Berlin
Nov. 8	Shakespeare	*The Merchant of Venice*	Deutsches Th., Berlin
Nov. 26	Kaiser	*The Fire in the Opera House*	Kleines Schauspielhaus, Berlin
Dec. 3	Hauptmann	*Michael Kramer*	Kleines Schauspielhaus, Berlin
Dec. 13	Tolstoy	*The Light That Shines in the Darkness*	Deutsches Th., Berlin
Dec. 21	Wedekind	*Pandora's Box*	Kleines Schauspielhaus, Berlin
Dec. 29	Unruh	*One Family*	Kammerspiele, Berlin

1919

Date	Author	Production	Theatre
Jan. 26	Lauckner	*The Fall of the Apostle Paul*	Kammerspiele, Berlin

Date	Author	Production	Theatre
Jan. 31	Kaiser	*From Morn to Mid-night*	Deutsches Th., Berlin
Feb. 2	Schönherr	*The Farce of Life*	Kammerspiele, Berlin
Feb. 27	Shakespeare	*As You Like It*	Deutsches Th., Berlin
Mar. 29	Rittner	*On the Way*	Kammerspiele, Berlin
Apr. 4	Hauptmann	*Henry of Aue*	Deutsches Th., Berlin
Apr. 10	Bahr	*The Star*	Kammerspiele, Berlin
Apr. 27	Lasker-Schüler	*The Wuppers*	Deutsches Th., Berlin
May 10	Lichnowsky	*The Children's Friend*	Kammerspiele, Berlin
May 25	Kokoschka	*Job*	Deutsches Th., Berlin
	Kokoschka	*The Burning Briar Bush*	
Oct. 10	Shakespeare	*Cymbeline*	Deutsches Th., Berlin
Oct. 17	Chekhov	*Ivanov*	Kammerspiele, Berlin
Nov. 7	Beer-Hofmann	*Jacob's Dream*	Deutsches Th., Berlin
Nov. 29	Aeschylus	*Oresteia*	Grosses Schauspiel-haus, Berlin
Dec. 9	Strindberg	*Advent*	Kammerspiele, Berlin
Dec. 16	Hauptmann	*And Pippa Dances*	Deutsches Th., Berlin

1920

Date	Author	Production	Theatre
Jan. 17	Shakespeare	*Hamlet*	Grosses Schauspiel-haus, Berlin
Jan. 25	Zweig	*Semael's Mission*	Kammerspiele, Berlin
Feb. 9	Nestroy	*Judith and Holofernes*	Grosses Schauspiel-haus, Berlin
Feb. 10	Bahr	*The Monster*	Kammerspiele, Berlin
Feb. 14	Rolland	*Danton*	Grosses Schauspiel-haus, Berlin
Mar. 4	Hauptmann	*Gabriel Schilling's Flight*	Kammerspiele, Berlin
Mar. 28	Hauptmann	*Helios*	Grosses Schauspiel-haus, Berlin
Apr. 3	Calderón	*The Fairy Lady*	Deutsches Th., Berlin
Apr. 13	Goethe	*Stella*	Kammerspiele, Berlin
Apr. 18	Hasenclever	*Antigone*	Grosses Schauspiel-haus, Berlin
Apr. 21	Kornfeld	*Heaven and Hell*	Deutsches Th., Berlin
May 25	Shakespeare	*Julius Caesar*	Grosses Schauspiel-haus, Berlin
Jun. 11	Aristophanes	*Lysistrata*	Grosses Schauspiel-haus, Berlin
Aug. 22	Hofmannsthal	*Everyman*	Domplatz, Salzburg
Sep. 17	Strindberg	*After the Fire*	Kammerspiele, Berlin
Sep. 29	Hauptmann	*Lonely Lives*	Deutsches Th., Berlin

Date	Author	Production	Theatre
Oct. 19	Tolstoy	*The First Distiller*	Kammerspiele, Berlin
	Gogol	*The Gamblers*	
Oct. 22	Goethe	*Urfaust*	Deutsches Th., Berlin
Nov. 5	Kaiser	*Europa*	Grosses Schauspielhaus, Berlin
Nov. 19–21	Goethe	*Urfaust*	Casino Th., Copenhagen
	Strindberg	*The Storm*	Dagmar Th., Copenhagen
	Goethe	*Stella*	
	Schnitzler	*The Big Scene*	
	Tolstoy	*The First Distiller*	
	Schiller	*Love and Intrigue*	
	Shakespeare	*The Merchant of Venice*	
	Strindberg	*The Ghost Sonata*	
	Strindberg	*The Pelican*	
	Strindberg	*The Dance of Death*	
Nov. 20	Rehfisch	*Chauffeur Martin*	Deutsches Th., Berlin
Nov. 27–29	Goethe	*Urfaust*	Lorensbergstheater, Göteborg
	Goethe	*Stella*	
	Strindberg	*The Pelican*	
Nov. 30–Dec. 5	Tolstoy	*The First Distiller*	National Th., Christiana
	Schnitzler	*The Big Scene*	
	Shakespeare	*The Merchant of Venice*	
Dec. 6–12	Strindberg	*The Dance of Death*	Royal Opera, Stockholm
	Schiller	*Love and Intrigue*	
	Strindberg	*The Storm*	Aarhus
Dec. 22	Shaw	*Caesar and Cleopatra*	Deutsches Th., Berlin

1921

Date	Author	Production	Theatre
Jan. 5	Hauptmann	*Florian Geyer*	Grosses Schauspielhaus, Berlin
	Hauptmann	*Florindo*	
Jan. 7	Hofmannsthal	*The Adventurer and the Singer*	Kammerspiele, Berlin
Jan. 21	Roessler	*The Pompous Hat*	Kammerspiele, Berlin
Feb. 5	Greban	*The Hobby*	Grosses Schauspielhaus, Berlin
Feb. 19	Schiller	*The Maid of Orleans*	Deutsches Th., Berlin
Feb. 24	Hasenclever	*Beyond*	Kammerspiele, Berlin

Date	Author	Production	Theatre
Mar. 4	Tagore	*The King of the Dark Chamber*	Kammerspiele, Berlin
Mar. 4	Offenbach	*Orpheus in the Underworld*	Casino Th., Copenhagen
Mar. 12	Shakespeare	*The Merchant of Venice*	Grosses Schauspielhaus, Berlin
Apr. 5	Büchner	*Woyzeck*	Deutsches Th., Berlin
Apr. 12	Stramm	*Powers*	Kammerspiele, Berlin
Apr. 19	Shakespeare	*A Midsummer Night's Dream*	Grosses Schauspielhaus, Berlin
May 2	Shaw	*Misalliance*	Kammerspiele, Berlin
Aug. 15	Hofmannsthal	*Everyman*	Domplatz, Salzburg
Sep. 4	Rolland	*Danton*	Grosses Schauspielhaus, Berlin
Sep. 7	Goethe	*Götz von Berlichingen*	Grosses Schauspielhaus, Berlin
Sep. 26	Schiller	*The Robbers*	Grosses Schauspielhaus, Berlin
Oct. 28	Strindberg	*A Dream Play*	Dramatiska Teater, Stockholm
Dec. 13	Strindberg	*A Dream Play*	Deutsches Th., Berlin
Dec. 17	Büchner	*Danton's Death*	Deutsches Th., Berlin
Dec. 31	Offenbach	*Orpheus in the Underworld*	Grosses Schauspielhaus, Berlin

1922

Date	Author	Production	Theatre
Jan. 30	Offenbach	*Orpheus in the Underworld*	Royal Opera, Stockholm
May 14	Hauptmann	*The Sunken Bell*	Grosses Schauspielhaus, Berlin
Jun. 30	Toller	*The Machine Wreckers*	Grosses Schauspielhaus, Berlin
Aug. 13	Hofmannsthal	*The Great Theatre of the World*	Kollegienkirche, Salzburg
Sep. 13	Goethe	*Clavigo*	Redoutensaal, Vienna
Sep. 16	Calderón	*The Fairy Lady*	Redoutensaal, Vienna
Oct. 16	Rey	*Beautiful Women*	Redoutensaal, Vienna
Oct. 22	Goethe	*Stella*	Redoutensaal, Vienna
Dec. 20	Lenormand	*The Failures*	Volkstheater, Vienna

1923

Date	Author	Production	Theatre
Aug. 20	Molière	*The Imaginary Invalid*	Leopoldskron, Salzburg
Aug. 21	Molière	*The Imaginary Invalid*	Stadttheater, Salzburg

Date	*Author*	*Production*	*Theatre*
1924			
Jan. 15	Vollmoeller	*The Miracle*	Century Th., New York
Apr. 1	Goldoni	*The Servant of Two Masters*	Th. in der Josefstadt, Vienna
Apr. 9	Schiller	*Love and Intrigue*	Th. in der Josefstadt, Vienna
Apr. 16	Hofmannsthal	*The Difficult Man*	Th. in der Josefstadt, Vienna
May 3	Calderón	*The Fairy Lady*	Th. in der Josefstadt, Vienna
May 26	Shakespeare	*The Merchant of Venice*	Th. in der Josefstadt, Vienna
Oct. 14	Rey	*Beautiful Women*	Th. in der Josefstadt, Vienna
Oct. 14	Shaw	*Saint Joan*	Deutsches Th., Berlin
Nov. 1	Goldoni	*The Servant of Two Masters*	Komödie, Berlin
Nov. 26	Molière	*The Imaginary Invalid*	Komödie, Berlin
Dec. 30	Pirandello	*Six Characters in Search of an Author*	Komödie, Berlin
Dec.– Jan. 1930	Vollmoeller	*The Miracle*	Cleveland, Cincinnati, Boston, St Louis, Chicago, Philadelphia, Kansas City, San Francisco, Los Angeles, Detroit, Milwaukee, St Paul, Dallas
1925			
Feb. 4	Shakespeare	*A Midsummer Night's Dream*	Th. in der Josefstadt, Vienna
Mar. 13	Shakespeare	*King Lear*	Th. in der Josefstadt, Vienna
Apr. 8	Galsworthy	*Loyalties*	Th. in der Josefstadt, Vienna
May 26	Werfel	*Juarez and Maximilian*	Th. in der Josefstadt, Vienna
Jun. 3	Goldoni	*The Servant of Two Masters*	Kammerspiele, Vienna
Aug. 13	Hofmannsthal	*The Great Theatre of the World*	Festspielhaus, Salzburg
Aug. 16	Vollmoeller	*The Miracle*	Festspielhaus, Salzburg
Aug. 25	Mell	*The Play of the Apostles*	Festspielhaus, Salzburg

Date	Author	Production	Theatre
Sept. 25	Galsworthy	*Loyalties*	Komödie, Berlin
Oct. 20	Klabund	*The Chalk Circle*	Deutsches Th., Berlin
Oct. 29	Mell	*The Play of the Apostles*	Kammerspiele, Berlin
Nov. 24	Maugham	*Rain*	Th. am Kurfürstendamm, Berlin
Dec. 23	Molnár	*Riviera*	Th. in der Josefstadt, Vienna

1926

Date	Author	Production	Theatre
Jan.	Molnár	*Riviera*	Magyar Szinház, Budapest
Jan. 29	Werfel	*Juarez and Maximilian*	Deutsches Th., Berlin
Mar. 5	Maugham	*Victoria*	Komödie, Berlin
Apr. 9	Kool	*Broadway*	Neues Deutsches Th., Prague
	Mozart	*The Magic Flute*	
May 4–6	Goldoni	*The Servant of Two Masters*	Basle, Bern, Zurcih
May 21	Bourdet	*The Prisoners*	Th. in der Josefstadt, Vienna
Jun. 23–Jul. 6	{ Bourdet { Turgeniev	*The Prisoners* *Natalie*	Magyar Szinház, Budapest
Aug. 8	Hofmannsthal	*Everyman*	Domplatz/Festspielhaus, Salzburg
Aug. 14	Gozzi	*Turandot*	Festspielhaus, Salzburg
Aug. 20	Goldoni	*The Servant of Two Masters*	Festspielhaus, Salzburg
Oct. 1	Langer	*The Ragged Edge*	Deutsches Th., Berlin
Oct. 20	Hauptmann	*Dorothea Angermann*	Th. in der Josefstadt, Vienna
Nov. 27	Maugham	*Victoria*	Th. in der Josefstadt, Vienna
Dec. 2–3	{ Tolstoy { Hofmannsthal	*The Living Corpse* *Everyman*	Basle, Zurich
Dec. 1–Jan. 15	{ Hofmannsthal { Vollmoeller	*Everyman* *The Miracle*	San Francisco

1927

Date	Author	Production	Theatre
Jan. 31–Mar. 5	{ Hofmannsthal { Vollmoeller	*Everyman* *The Miracle*	Los Angeles
Feb. 19–20	Bourdet	*The Prisoners*	Basle, Zurich
Apr. 4–8	Verneuil	*Merry-Go-Round*	Zurich, Basle, Bern

Date	Author	Production	Theatre
May 11	Bernard	*The Good Comrade*	Th. in der Josefstadt, Vienna
May 26	Vollmoeller	*The Miracle*	Városi Szinház, Budapest
Jun. 1	Langer	*The Ragged Edge*	Th. in der Josefstadt, Vienna
Jun. 2	Vollmoeller	*The Miracle*	Prager Th., Prague
Jun. 7	Vollmoeller	*The Miracle*	Circus Renz, Vienna
Jul. 30	Hofmannsthal	*Everyman*	Domplatz/Festspielhaus, Salzburg
Aug. 6	Shakespeare	*A Midsummer Night's Dream*	Festspielhaus, Salzburg
Aug. 12	Schiller	*Love and Intrigue*	Festspielhaus, Salzburg
Sep. 3	Bourdet	*The Prisoners*	Komödie, Berlin
Oct. 18	Hauptmann	*Dorothea Angermann*	Deutsches Th., Berlin
Nov. 17	Shakespeare	*A Midsummer Night's Dream*	Century Th., New York
Dec. 7	Hofmannsthal	*Everyman*	Century Th., New York
Dec. 20	Büchner	*Danton's Death*	Century Th., New York

1928

Date	Author	Production	Theatre
Jan. 2	Langer	*The Ragged Edge*	Cosmopolitan Th., New York
Jan. 9	Goldoni	*The Servant of Two Masters*	Cosmopolitan Th., New York
	Tolstoy	*The Cause of It All*	
Jan. 16	Schiller	*Love and Intrigue*	Cosmopolitan Th., New York
Jan. 23	Tolstoy	*The Living Corpse* [Redemption]	Cosmopolitan Th., New York
Apr. 13	Guitry	*Desirée*	Vigszinház, Budapest
May 15	Géraldy	*Robert and Marianne*	Vigszinház, Budapest
Jun. 9	Watters and Hopkins	*Artists*	Deutsches Th., Berlin
Jul. 26	Billinger	*The Perchten Play*	Festspielhaus, Salzburg
Jul. 27	Hofmannsthal	*Everyman*	Domplatz/Festspielhaus, Salzburg
Jul. 28	Goethe	*Iphigenia in Tauris*	Festspielhaus, Salzburg
Aug. 8	Schiller	*The Robbers*	Festspielhaus, Salzburg
Oct. 25	Shakespeare	*Romeo and Juliet*	Berliner Th., Berlin
Oct. 31	Tolstoy	*The Living Corpse*	Th. in der Josefstadt, Vienna
Nov. 11	Schiffer and Spoliansky	*It's in the Air*	Schauspielhaus, Zurich
Nov. 29	Géraldy	*Robert and Marianne*	Stadttheater, Basle
Nov. 30	Goethe	*Iphigenia in Tauris*	Stadttheater, Basle

Date	Author	Production	Theatre
Dec. 2	Géraldy	*Robert and Marianne*	Stadttheater, Zurich
Dec. 3	Goethe	*Iphigenia in Tauris*	Stadttheater, Zurich

1929

May 19	Bourdet	*The Prisoners*	Deutsches Th., Berlin
Jun. 4–13	Büchner	*Danton's Death*	Rathaus Arcades, Vienna
Jun. 8	Strauss	*Die Fledermaus*	Deutsches Th., Berlin
Jun. 19–	{ Schiller	*Love and Intrigue*	Festspiele, Munich
Jul.	{ Maugham	*Victoria*	
Aug. 4	Hofmannsthal	*Everyman*	Domplatz/Festspielhaus, Salzburg
Oct. 29	Shaw	*The Apple Cart*	Deutsches Th., Berlin
Nov. 11	Hamsun	*In the Grip of Life*	Komödie, Berlin

1930

Jan. 11	Shaw	*The Apple Cart*	Th. in der Josefstadt, Vienna
Jan. 24	Maugham	*Victoria*	Deutsches Th., Berlin
Mar. 10	Bruckner	*The Creature*	Komödie, Berlin
Apr. 6	Strauss	*Die Fledermaus*	Th. Royal, Copenhagen
May 13	Unruh	*Phaea*	Deutsches Th., Berlin
Jun. 28	Strauss	*Die Fledermaus*	Deutsches Th., Berlin
Aug. 1	Hofmannsthal	*Everyman*	Domplatz/Festspielhaus, Salzburg
Aug. 3	Schiller	*Love and Intrigue*	Festspielhaus, Salzburg
Aug. 10	Maugham	*Victoria*	Festspielhaus, Salzburg
Aug. 12	Goldoni	*The Servant of Two Masters*	Festspielhaus, Salzburg
Sep.	Goldoni	*The Servant of Two Masters*	Komödie, Berlin
Sep.	Hofmannsthal	*The Difficult Man*	Komödie, Berlin
Sep.	Shaw	*The Apple Cart*	Deutsches Th., Berlin
Sep.	Shakespeare	*A Midsummer Night's Dream*	Deutsches Th., Berlin
Nov. 1	Bruckner	*Elizabeth of England*	Deutsches Th., Berlin
Dec. 3	Goldoni	*The Servant of Two Masters*	Kammerspiele, Berlin

1931

Jan. 27	Bourdet	*The Weaker Sex*	Th. am Kurfürstendamm, Berlin

Date	Author	Production	Theatre
Mar.	Zuckmayer	*The Captain from Copenick*	Deutsches Th., Berlin
Mar. 10	Bourdet	*The Weaker Sex*	Oscar Th., Stockholm
Apr. 26	Goldoni	*The Servant of Two Masters*	Schauspielhaus, Zurich
Apr. 27	Maugham	*Victoria*	Schauspielhaus, Zurich
Apr. 28	Maugham	*Victoria*	Stadttheater, Bern
May 1	Goldoni	*The Servant of Two Masters*	Stadttheater, Basle
May 2	Maugham	*Victoria*	Stadttheater, Basle
May 7	Goldoni	*The Servant of Two Masters*	Fővárosi Operettszin- ház, Budapest
May 8	Bourdet	*The Weaker Sex*	Th. in der Josefstadt, Vienna
Jun. 15	Offenbach	*La Belle Hélène*	Komödie, Berlin
Jun. 21	Strauss	*Die Fledermaus*	Nationaloper, Riga
Jul. 26	Hofmannsthal	*Everyman*	Domplatz/Festspiel- haus, Salzburg
Jul. 26	Shakespeare	*Twelfth Night*	Leopoldskron, Salz- burg
Jul. 28	Goldoni	*The Servant of Two Masters*	Festspielhaus, Salzburg
Aug. 2	Hofmannsthal	*The Difficult Man*	Festspielhaus, Salzburg
Aug. 13	Goethe	*Stella*	Festspielhaus, Salzburg
Aug.	Strauss	*Die Fledermaus*	Copenhagen
	Offenbach	*Orpheus in the Underworld*	Stockholm, Riga
	Goldoni	*The Servant of Two Masters*	Riga
Autumn	Maugham	*Victoria*	Fővárosi Operettszin- ház, Budapest
Nov. 11	Shakespeare	*Twelfth Night*	Th. in der Josefstadt, Vienna
Nov. 28	Offenbach	*Tales of Hoffmann*	Grosses Schauspiel- haus, Berlin
Dec. 25	Offenbach	*La Belle Hélène*	Opera House, Man- chester

1932

Date	Author	Production	Theatre
Jan. 30	Offenbach	*La Belle Hélène*	Adelphi Th., London
Feb. 16	Hauptmann	*Before Sunset*	Deutsches Th., Berlin
Mar.	Offenbach	*Orpheus in the Underworld*	Nationaloper, Riga
Apr. 9	Vollmoeller	*The Miracle*	Lyceum Th., London
May 11	Schiller	*Love and Intrigue*	Schauspielhaus, Zurich
May 12	Goldoni	*The Servant of two Masters*	Schauspielhaus, Zurich

Date	Author	Production	Theatre
Jun. 6	Offenbach	*La Belle Hélène*	Volksoper, Vienna
Jun. 10	Deval	*Mademoiselle*	Th. in der Josefstadt, Vienna
Jul. 31	Hofmannsthal	*Everyman*	Domplatz/Festspielhaus, Salzburg
Nov.	Kleist	*The Prince of Homburg*	Deutsches Th., Berlin
	Offenbach	*La Belle Hélène*	London, Manchester
	Schiller	*Love and Intrigue*	Zurich
	Goldoni	*The Servant of Two Masters*	Rome, Milan

1933

Date	Author	Production	Theatre
Mar. 1	Hofmannsthal	*The Great Theatre of the World*	Deutsches Th., Berlin
Mar. 17	Goethe	*Faust I*	Felsenreitschule, Salzburg
May 31	Shakespeare	*A Midsummer Night's Dream*	Boboli Gardens, Florence
Jun. 15	Shakespeare	*A Midsummer Night's Dream*	South Park, Headington, Oxford
Jul. 30	Hofmannsthal	*Everyman*	Domplatz/Festspielhaus, Salzburg
Aug. 17	Goethe	*Faust I*	Felsenreitschule/Festspielhaus, Salzburg
Sep. 4	Goethe	*Faust I*	Th. in der Josefstadt, Vienna
Nov. 28	Strauss	*Die Fledermaus*	Th. Pigalle, Paris
Nov. 29	Schnitzler	*Farewell Supper*	Magyar Szinház, Budapest
	Schnitzler	*Light o' Love*	
Nov. 30	Jaráy	*Is Geraldine an Angel?*	Magyar Szinház, Budapest

1934

Date	Author	Production	Theatre
Jan. 1– May 24	Goldoni	*The Servant of Two Masters*	Th. Royal, The Hague; Stadttheater, Amsterdam; Grosses Schauspielhaus, Rotterdam; Stadttheater, Haarlem; Stadttheater, Arnhem; Kursaal, Scheveningen; Stadttheater, Utrecht; Rembrandttheater, Eindhoven
	Schiller	*Maria Stuart*	
	Pirandello	*Six Characters in Search of an Author*	

Date	Author	Production	Theatre
Jan. 31	Goldoni	*The Servant of Two Masters*	Th. Royal, Antwerp
Feb. 17	Strauss	*Die Fledermaus*	Milan, Rome, San Remo
Mar.	Cocteau	*La Voix humaine*	Th. in der Josefstadt, Vienna
	Pirandello	*Six Characters in Search of an Author*	Th. in der Josefstadt, Vienna; Milan
	Schiller	*Maria Stuart*	Th. in der Josefstadt, Vienna; Milan
Mar. 31	Schiller	*Maria Stuart*	Neues Deutsches Th., Prague
Apr. 1	Pirandello	*Six Characters in Search of an Author*	Neues Deutsches Th., Prague
May 7	Pirandello	*Six Characters in Search of an Author*	Schauspielhaus, Zurich
May 13	Pirandello	*Six Characters in Search of an Author*	Stadttheater, Basle
Jul. 18	Shakespeare	*The Merchant of Venice*	Campo San Trovaso, Venice
Jul. 29	Hofmannsthal	*Everyman*	Domplatz/Festspielhaus, Salzburg
Aug. 7	Goethe	*Faust I*	Felsenreitschule/Festspielhaus, Salzburg
Sep. 17	Shakespeare	*A Midsmmer Night's Dream*	Hollywood Bowl, Los Angeles
Oct. 1	Shakespeare	*A Midsummer Night's Dream*	Opera House, San Francisco
Oct. 13	Shakespeare	*A Midsummer Night's Dream*	Faculty Glade and Greek Th., Berkeley
Nov. 15	Shakespeare	*A Midsummer Night's Dream*	Auditorium Th., Chicago
Dec. 8	Shakespeare	*A Midsummer Night's Dream*	Auditorium Th., Milwaukee
Dec.	Shakespeare	*A Midsummer Night's Dream*	Municipal Auditorium/Opera House, St Louis

1935

Date	Author	Production	Theatre
Feb. 28	Blum	*The Princess up the Ladder*	Fővárosi Operettszinház, Budapest
Apr. 6	Guitry	*His New Will*	Vigszinház, Budapest
Jul. 28	Hofmannsthal	*Everyman*	Domplatz/Festspielhaus, Salzburg
Aug. 2	Goethe	*Faust I*	Felsenreitschule/Festspielhaus, Salzburg

Date	Author	Production	Theatre
Summer	Shakespeare	*The Merchant of Venice*	Campo San Trovaso, Venice
Oct. 9	Shakespeare	*A Midsummer Night's Dream* (film)	{ Hollywood Th., New York / Adelphi Th., London

1936

Jul. 26	Hofmannsthal	*Everyman*	Domplatz/Festspielhaus, Salzburg
Jul. 30	Goethe	*Faust I*	Felsenreitschule/ Festspielhaus, Salzburg

1937

Jan. 7	Werfel	*The Eternal Road*	Manhattan Opera House, New York
Jul. 25	Hofmannsthal	*Everyman*	Domplatz/Festspielhaus, Salzburg
Jul. 29	Goethe	*Faust I*	Felsenreitschule/ Festspielhaus, Salzburg
Oct. 5	Werfel	*In One Night*	Th. in der Josefstadt, Vienna

1938

Aug. 7	Maeterlinck	*Sister Beatrice*	Hollywood, Los Angeles
Aug. 15	Maeterlinck	*Sister Beatrice*	Hollywood, Los Angeles
Aug. 23	Goethe	*Faust I*	Pilgrimage Th., Los Angeles
Aug. 28	Goethe	*Faust I*	Civic Auditorium, San Francisco
Oct. 24	Maeterlinck	*Sister Beatrice*	Hollywood, Los Angeles
Dec. 12	Wilder	*The Merchant of Yonkers*	Colonial Th., Boston
Dec. 28	Nestroy	*He Wants to Play a Joke*	Guild Th., New York

1939

Feb. 9–10	Maeterlinck	*Sister Beatrice*	Lobero Th., Santa Barbara
Feb. 25	Pirandello	*Six Characters in Search of an Author*	5939 Sunset Blvd, Los Angeles

Date	Author	Production	Theatre
May 31	Goldoni	The Servant of Two Masters [At Your Service]	Assistance League Playhouse, Los Angeles
Summer	Maeterlinck	Sister Beatrice	San Francisco
Sep. 10	Shakespeare	A Midsummer Night's Dream	5939 Sunset Blvd, Los Angeles

1940

Date	Author	Production	Theatre
Jan. 7	Goldoni	The Servant of Two Masters	Geary Th., San Francisco
Jan. 8	Maeterlinck	Sister Beatrice	Geary Th., San Francisco
Jan. 9	Pirandello	Six Characters in Search of an Author	Geary Th., San Francisco
Jan. 18	Maugham	Victoria [Too Many Husbands]	Belasco Th., Los Angeles
Mar. 13	Hofmannsthal	Everyman	Hollywood, Los Angeles
Jun.	Quintero	Fortunato	Hollywood, Los Angeles

1941

Date	Author	Production	Theatre
Jan.	Wilder	The Merchant of Yonkers	Max Reinhardt Th., Hollywood
May 8	Hofmannsthal	Everyman	Th. Friendship House, New York
Jul. 2	Shakespeare	"Shakespeare's Women, Clowns and Songs"	Max Reinhardt Th., Hollywood
Aug.	Winsloe	Girls in Uniform	Max Reinhardt Th., Hollywood
Nov. 29	Kataev	Squaring the Circle	Max Reinhardt Th., Hollywood

1942

Date	Author	Production	Theatre
Oct. 28	Strauss	Die Fledermaus [Rosalinda]	44th St. Th., New York

1943

Date	Author	Production	Theatre
May	Strauss	Die Fledermaus	Imperial Th., New York
May 4	Irwin Shaw	Sons and Soldiers	Morosco Th., New York
Autumn	Strauss	Die Fledermaus	44th St. Th., New York

Notes

1 AN EXPLOSION OF IDEAS IN THE THEATRE

1 Hermann Bahr, "The makings of Max Reinhardt," *New York Times*, 30 December 1923, p. 10.
2 W. Bridges-Adams, "The Reinhardt touch," *The Listener*, 10 June 1954, p. 1002.
3 Allan S. Jackson in *Theatre Studies 20* (Columbus, Ohio, 1973–4), p. 54.
4 Cecil W. Davies, *Theatre for the People: The Story of the Volksbühne* (Austin, Texas, 1977), p. 69.
5 George E. Wellwarth and Alfred G. Brooks, eds., *Max Reinhardt, 1873–1973: A Centennial Festschrift* (Binghamton, New York, 1973), p. 129.
6 Herbert Ihering, *Reinhardt, Jessner, Piscator oder Klassikertod?* (Berlin, 1929), p. 12.
7 Sheldon Cheney, *The New Movement in the Theatre* (New York, 1914), p. 29.
8 Ihering, *Reinhardt, Jessner, Piscator*, p. 12. Others who also considered Reinhardt to be a creator of "noble kitsch" were Karl Kraus and Alfred Kerr.
9 Wellwarth and Brooks, *Max Reinhardt, 1873–1973*, p. 87.
10 Jackson in *Theatre Studies 20*, p. 50.
11 Georg Fuchs, *Revolution in the Theatre: Conclusions Concerning the Munich Artists' Theatre*, translated and adapted by Constance Connor Kuhn (Ithaca, New York, 1959), p. xvii.
12 Paul Raabe, ed., *The Era of Expressionism*, trans. J. M. Ritchie (London, 1974), p. 297.
13 Cheney, *The New Movement*, pp. 58–9.
14 Wellwarth and Brooks, *Max Reinhardt, 1873–1973*, foreword.
15 Bahr, *New York Times*, 30 December 1923, p. 10.
16 Roy Pascal, *From Naturalism to Expressionism: German Literature and Society, 1880–1918* (London, 1973), pp. 281–2.
17 Harley Granville-Barker, *The Times*, 19 November 1910.
18 "Es gibt keine Form des Theaters, die die einzig wahre künstlerische Form wäre": Hugo Fetting, ed., *Max Reinhardt Schriften* (Berlin, 1974), p. 336. Afterwards referred to as "*Schriften*."
19 In Berlin at the Neues Theater, 3 March 1904; in London at the Court Theatre, 26 April 1904.
20 Adolphe Appia, *Die Musik und die Inszenierung* (Munich, 1899) and Edward Gordon Craig, *On the Art of the Theatre* (London, 1911).
21 H. F. Garten, *Modern German Drama* (Fair Lawn, New Jersey, 1959), pp. 84–5.
22 "Heute und für alle Zeiten muss der Mensch in Mittelpunkt aller Schauspielkunst stehen, der Mensch als Schauspieler": *Schriften*, p. 314.
23 Felix Hollaender and Arthur Kahane, eds., *Blätter des Deutschen Theaters* (Berlin, 1911–14), translated in Huntly Carter, *The Theatre of Max Reinhardt* (London, 1914), p. 121.
24 Bridges-Adams, *The Listener*, 10 June 1954, p. 1002.

2 BEGINNINGS IN IMPRESSIONISTIC REALISM

1 H. I. Pilikian, "Max Reinhardt" in *Encyclopaedia Britannica*, vol. 15 (Chicago, 1978), p. 581.

2 Hans Rothe, ed., *Max Reinhardt: 25 Jahre Deutsches Theater* (Munich, 1930), appendix.
3 Ernst Stern, *My Life, My Stage*, trans. Edward Fitzgerald (London, 1951), pp. 74–5.
4 Frank Washburn-Freund, "The evolution of Reinhardt" in Oliver M. Sayler, ed., *Max Reinhardt and His Theatre* (New York, 1924), pp. 52–3. Afterwards referred to as "Sayler."
5 Siegfried Jacobsohn, *Max Reinhardt* (Berlin, 1921), p. 11.
6 *Ibid.*, pp. 11–13.

3 INTO SYMBOLIST DRAMA

1 Mordecai Gorelik, *New Theatres for Old* (New York, 1940), p. 180.
2 In 1905 Reinhardt had asked Craig to collaborate with him over the production of Hofmannsthal's *Electra* in Berlin. Craig drew a series of designs, but demanded an autonomy that Reinhardt was not prepared to grant.
3 William Archer quoted in Huntly Carter, *The Theatre of Max Reinhardt* (London, 1914), p. 87.
4 Sheldon Cheney, *The New Movement in the Theatre* (New York, 1914), p. 55.
5 "Stark und eigenartig." See the letters of August 1902 and 21 July 1904 in *Schriften*, pp. 77 and 85.
6 Letter to Friedrich von Oppeln Bronikowski in Sayler, p. 330.
7 Ernst Stern, *My Life, My Stage*, trans. Edward Fitzgerald (London, 1951), p. 86.
8 *Ibid.*, p. 87.
9 *Ibid.*, p. 89.
10 *The Times*, 22 August 1911.
11 *Ibid.*, 20 February 1911.
12 *Ibid.*, 20 February 1911.
13 W. Bridges-Adams, "The Reinhardt Touch," *The Listener*, 10 June 1954, p. 1002.
14 12 November 1912.
15 12 November 1912.

4 EXPRESSIONIST EXPERIMENT

1 See letter of 16 October 1906 in *Schriften*, pp. 97–8.
2 See letter of 7 October 1908 in *Schriften*, pp. 100–1.
3 See Kela Kvam, *Max Reinhardt og Strindbergs visionaere dramatik* (Copenhagen, 1974).
4 Siegfried Jacobsohn, *Max Reinhardt* (Berlin, 1921), p. 80.
5 See Kenneth Macgowan and Robert Edmond Jones, *Continental Stagecraft* (New York, 1922), chapter ix.
6 Gusti Adler, *Max Reinhardt: Sein Leben* (Salzburg, 1964), p. 65.
7 Ashley Dukes, *The Scene Is Changed* (London, 1942), p. 52.
8 Jacobsohn, *Max Reinhardt*, p. 82.
9 Dukes, *The Scene Is Changed*, p. 52.
10 Walter H. Sokel, ed., *An Anthology of German Expressionist Drama* (New York, 1963), p. xv.
11 Rudolf Frank, *Das neue Theater* (Berlin, 1928), p. 32.
12 Edward Gordon Craig's *The Art of the Theatre* was first published in 1905 in German.
13 Denis Calandra, "Georg Kaiser's *From Morn to Midnight*: the nature of expressionist performance" in *Theatre Quarterly 21* (Spring 1976), pp. 45–54.
14 *Theaterkalender auf das Jahr 1914*, p. 55. Quoted in Calandra, "Georg Kaiser's *From Morn to Midnight*," p. 48.
15 *Das junge Deutschland* (Berlin, January 1918), pp. 1–13.

16 Trans. Richard Samuel in Richard Samuel and R. Hinton Thomas, *Expressionism in German Life, Literature and the Theatre, 1910–1924* (Philadelphia, 1939), p. 67.
17 *Ibid.*, pp. 67–8.
18 Trans. Walter H. and Jacqueline Sokel in Walter H. Sokel, ed., *An Anthology of German Expressionist Drama* (New York, 1963), pp. 41–6.
19 See R. W. Last, ed., *Affinities: Essays in German and English Literature* (London, 1971).
20 21 December 1927.
21 Ernst Stern and Heinz Herald, eds., *Reinhardt und seine Bühne* (Berlin, 1918), p. 87, translated in Stern, *My Life, My Stage* (London, 1951), pp. 161–2; reprinted in Stern, *Bühnenbildner bei Max Reinhardt* (Berlin, 1955), p. 125.
22 Jacobsohn, *Max Reinhardt*, p. 133.
23 Stern and Herald, *Reinhardt und seine Bühne*, pp. 88–91, translated in Stern, *My Life, My Stage*, pp. 162–3.
24 Wolfram Viehweg in Maurice Benn, *The Drama of Revolt: A Critical Study of Georg Büchner* (Cambridge, 1976), p. 112.
25 Trans. Geoffrey Dunlop, *The Plays of Georg Büchner* (London, 1952).
26 So Klaus Pfützner considered in 1973: see *Schriften*, p. 406.

5 REINHARDT'S SHAKESPEARE

1 The following are Reinhardt's performances of Shakespeare, 1905–30:

A Midsummer Night's Dream	427	*The Merry Wives of Windsor*	64
The Merchant of Venice	363	*As You Like It*	63
Twelfth Night	291	*The Comedy of Errors*	59
Hamlet	227	*Henry IV, Part I*	43
The Winter's Tale	199	*Macbeth*	42
Romeo and Juliet	172	*Henry IV, Part II*	40
The Taming of the Shrew	102	*Troilus and Cressida*	35
Othello	99	*The Tempest*	30
King Lear	94	*Cymbeline*	14
Much Ado About Nothing	74	*Richard II*	11
Julius Caesar	69	*Coriolanus*	9

(Taken from Hans Rothe, ed., *Max Reinhardt: 25 Jahre Deutsches Theater*, Munich, 1930.)
2 "Rede über den Schauspieler" in *Schriften*, p. 324.
3 H. K. Moderwell, *The Theatre of Today* (New York, 1915), p. 129.
4 See p. 24.
5 Kenneth Macgowan and Robert Edmond Jones, *Continental Stagecraft* (New York, 1922), p. 112.
6 Rudolph Kommer, "The Magician of Leopoldskron" in Sayler, pp. 6–7.
7 "Aus dem Regiebuch *Ein Sommernachtstraum*" in *Schriften*, p. 270.
8 Ernst Stern and Heinz Herald, eds., *Reinhardt und seine Bühne* (Berlin, 1918), p. 38.
9 Siegfried Jacobsohn, *Max Reinhardt* (Berlin, 1921), p. 1.
10 Kenneth Macgowan, *The Theatre of Tomorrow* (New York, 1921), p. 67.
11 Frank Washburn-Freund, "The evolution of Reinhardt" in Sayler, p. 52.
12 Jacobsohn, *Max Reinhardt*, p. 1.
13 27 November 1927.
14 *Schriften*, p. 268.
15 Ernst Stern, *My Life, My Stage*, trans. Edward Fitzgerald (London, 1951), p. 63.
16 *Schriften*, p. 270.
17 Jacobsohn, *Max Reinhardt*, p. 1.

18 Stern and Herald, *Reinhardt und seine Bühne*, p. 43.
19 *Schriften*, pp. 271–2.
20 Felix Felton, "Max Reinhardt in England" in *Theatre Research*, vol. 5, no. 3, ed. Hans Knudsen (London, 1963), pp. 141–2.
21 16 June 1933.
22 15 June 1933.
23 23 June 1933.
24 Felton, "Max Reinhardt in England," p. 142.
25 "Gespräch über Reinhardt mit Hugo von Hofmannsthal, Alfred Roller und Bruno Walter" (1910) in *Schriften*, p. 383.
26 Georg Brandes in "An international symposium on Reinhardt" in Sayler, p. 330.
27 Jacobsohn, *Max Reinhardt*, p. 4.
28 Dieter Hoffmeier, "Versuch über Reinhardt" in *Schriften*, p. 433.
29 Macgowan and Jones, *Continental Stagecraft*, p. 112.
30 Franz Hadamowsky, ed., *Max Reinhardt: Ausgewählte Briefe, Reden, Schriften und Szenen aus Regiebüchern* (Vienna, 1963), pp. 153–63.
31 Marvin Rosenberg, *The Masks of Macbeth* (Berkeley, California, 1978), pp. 83–4.
32 Manfred Grossmann, ed., *Max Reinhardts Regiebuch zu Macbeth, Schweize Theater Jahrbuch 31 and 32* (Basle, 1965–6), pp. 19–25, 32–8, 49–55, 80–99.

6 A STYLE FOR EVERY PLAY

1 In Sayler, p. 139.
2 The critic Schultze-Naumburg, quoted by Stern in *My Life, My Stage*, trans. Edward Fitzgerald (London, 1951), p. 220.
3 Gusti Adler in George E. Wellwarth and Alfred G. Brooks, eds., *Max Reinhardt, 1873–1973: A Centennial Festschrift* (Binghamton, New York, 1973), p. 20.
4 *Schriften*, pp. 278–87.
5 *The Times*, 21 November 1910, p. 12.
6 In Wellwarth and Brooks, *Max Reinhardt, 1873–1973*, p. 20.
7 Huntly Carter, *The Theatre of Max Reinhardt* (London, 1914), p. 256.
8 Edda Leisler and Gisela Prossnitz, eds., *Max Reinhardt und die Welt des Commedia dell'arte* (Salzburg, 1970).
9 Leonhard M. Fiedler, *Max Reinhardt und Molière* (Salzburg, 1972), p. 54, quoting footnote 112.
10 H. I. Pilikian, "Max Reinhardt" in *Encyclopaedia Britannica*, vol. 15 (Chicago, 1978), pp. 580–1.
11 Carter, *The Theatre of Max Reinhardt*, p. 220.
12 John Martin-Harvey, *Autobiography* (London, 1933), p. 398.
13 16 January 1912.
14 16 January 1912.
15 16 January 1912.
16 Martin-Harvey, *Autobiography*, p. 393.
17 16 January 1912.
18 20 January 1912.
19 21 January 1912.
20 See Bernard F. Dukore and Daniel C. Gerould, eds., *Avant-Garde Drama: A Casebook, 1918–1939* (New York, 1976), p. 490.
21 Carter, *The Theatre of Max Reinhardt*, p. 210.
22 21 January 1912.
23 Martin-Harvey, *Autobiography*, p. 405.
24 *The Morning Post*, 16 January 1912.
25 20 January 1912.

26 Letter from Berlin in 1910, in C. B. Purdom, *Harley Granville-Barker, Man of the Theatre, Dramatist and Scholar* (London, 1955), p. 115.
27 Reproduced in Carter, *The Theatre of Max Reinhardt*, pp. 221–2.

7 THE BAROQUE SPECTACLES

1 William Poel, *Monthly Letters* (London, 1929), p. 84.
2 See Allardyce Nicoll, *English Drama, 1900–1930* (Cambridge, 1973), p. 93.
3 "Reinhardt über sein *Mirakel* und seine Zukunftspläne," an interview in 1914, in *Schriften*, p. 261.
4 "Auf der Suche nach dem lebendigen Theater" (1924), in *Schriften*, p. 189.
5 H. I. Pilikian, "Max Reinhardt" in *Encyclopaedia Britannica*, vol. 15 (Chicago, 1978), p. 580.
6 Hugo von Hofmannsthal, *Selected Plays, and Libretti*, ed. Michael Hamburger (New York, 1963), introduction, p. xliii.
7 Franz Hadamowsky, *Reinhardt und Salzburg* (Salzburg, 1964), p. 33.
8 Hugo von Hofmannsthal, *Vorspiel für ein Puppentheater* (1906), quoted in *Selected Plays*, ed. Hamburger, p. xxi.
9 Hadamowsky, *Reinhardt und Salzburg*, p. 39.
10 Hugo von Hofmannsthal, "Reinhardt as an international force," trans. Sidney Howard, in *Sayler*, pp. 25–6.
11 Excerpted in Franz Hadamowsky, ed., *Max Reinhardt: Ausgewählte Briefe, Reden, Schriften und Szenen aus Regiebüchern* (Vienna, 1963), pp. 168–72.
12 In the Max Reinhardt Archive, the State University of New York, Binghamton, New York.
13 21 September 1936, in C. B. Purdom, *Harley Granville-Barker, Man of the Theatre, Dramatist and Scholar* (London, 1955), p. 246.
14 Hofmannsthal, *Selected Plays*, ed. Hamburger, pp. xlii–xliii.
15 *New York Times*, 9 May 1941.
16 See especially Sayler, appendix I and Huntly Carter, *The Theatre of Max Reinhardt* (London, 1914), pp. 223ff.
17 John Palmer in *The Saturday Review*, 20 January 1912, p. 75.
18 Ernst Stern, *My Life, My Stage* (London, 1951), p. 96.
19 25 December 1911.
20 10 January 1912, p. 32.
21 Norman Bel Geddes, *Miracle in the Evening: An Autobiography*, ed. William Kelley (New York, 1960), p. 275.
22 Stern, *My Life, My Stage*, p. 92.
23 *Ibid.*, p. 96.
24 Carter, *The Theatre of Max Reinhardt*, p. 232.
25 10 January 1912, p. 32.
26 30 December 1911, p. 827.
27 *New York Times*, 16 January 1924.
28 See Geddes, *Miracle in the Evening*, p. 299.
29 8 December 1927.
30 11 April 1932.
31 11 April 1932.
32 10 April 1932.
33 Hofmannsthal, *Selected Plays*, ed. Hamburger, p. xli.
34 Hofmannsthal, translated by Vernon Watkins, in *Selected Plays*, ed. Hamburger, pp. 88–9.
35 Alfred Schwarz, *From Büchner to Beckett: Dramatic Theory and the Modes of Tragic Drama* (Athens, Ohio, 1978), p. 234.

36 Eric Gort, "Masks for dance and theatre," *Direction*, vol. 4, no. 7 (Darien, Connecticut, January 1941), p. 12.
37 Hugo von Hofmannsthal, "The repertory of festival" in *Sayler*, p. 203.
38 Gort, "Masks for dance and theatre," p. 12.
39 Hofmannsthal, translated by Vernon Watkins, in *Selected Plays*, ed. Hamburger, p. 154.
40 "Auf der Suche nach dem lebendigen Theater" (1924), in *Schriften*, p. 190.
41 Hofmannsthal, "The repertory of festival" in *Sayler*, pp. 207–8.

8 REINHARDT, MAN OF THE THEATRE

1 Robert F. Willson, Jr., "Ill met by moonlight: Reinhardt's *A Midsummer Night's Dream* and musical screwball comedy," *Journal of Popular Film*, nos. 5–6 (Summer 1977), pp. 185–97.
2 See William W. Melnitz in George E. Wellwarth and Alfred G. Brooks, eds., *Max Reinhardt, 1873–1973: A Centennial Festschrift* (Binghamton, New York, 1973), p. 100.
3 Gusti Adler, *Max Reinhardt: Sein Leben* (Salzburg, 1964), p. 42.
4 Siegfried Jacobsohn, *Max Reinhardt* (Berlin, 1921), p. 11.
5 Adler, *Max Reinhardt: Sein Leben*, p. 43.
6 Anna Miller, *The Independent Theatre of Europe, 1887 to the Present* (New York, 1931), p. 139.
7 Gottfried Reinhardt, *The Genius: A Memoir of Max Reinhardt by His Son* (New York, 1979), p. 365.
8 Meyer Weisgal, *So Far: An Autobiography* (New York, 1971), p. 141.
9 Arthur Kahane, "Glossen zum Theater der Fünftausend" in Felix Hollaender and Arthur Kahane, eds., *Blätter des Deutschen Theaters* (Berlin, 1911–14), translated in Huntly Carter, *The Theatre of Max Reinhardt* (London, 1914), pp. 122–3.
10 *Ibid.*, p. 124.
11 Kenneth Macgowan and Robert Edmond Jones, *Continental Stagecraft* (New York, 1922), p. 163.
12 *Ibid.*, pp. 164–7.
13 Arthur Kahane in Carter, *The Theatre of Max Reinhardt*, p. 124.
14 E. J. Dent, "The stage picture" in Sayler, pp. 142–3.
15 Macgowan and Jones, *Continental Stagecraft*, p. 185.
16 Heinz Herald, "The Kammerspiele" in Sayler, p. 149.
17 21 November, 1910. See also Harley Granville-Barker, "Two German theatres," *Fortnightly Review*, no. 89 (London, January 1911), pp. 60–70, for a description of the Deutsches Theater repertory.
18 Ben Iden Payne, *A Life in a Wooden O: Memoirs of the Theatre* (New Haven, 1977), p. 81.
19 Arthur Kahane, "Reinhardt as stage director" in Sayler, p. 85.
20 Heinz Herald, "Reinhardt at Rehearsal" in Sayler, p. 118.
21 Norman Bel Geddes, *Miracle in the Evening: An Autobiography*, ed. William Kelley (New York, 1960), p. 295.
22 Cecil W. Davies, *Theatre for the People: The Story of the Volksbühne* (Austin, Texas, 1977), p. 69.
23 *Theatre Research*, vol. 5, no. 3, ed. Hans Knudsen (London, 1963), p. 139.
24 In Davies, *Theatre for the People*, p. 68.
25 Wellwarth and Brooks, eds., *Max Reinhardt, 1873–1973*, p. 25.
26 Gottfried Reinhardt, *The Genius*, p. 122.
27 Frank Washburn-Freund, "The evolution of Reinhardt" in Sayler, p. 56.
28 Carter, *The Theatre of Max Reinhardt*, p. 80.

29 Gottfried Reinhardt, *The Genius*, p. 363.
30 Bertold Held, "Massenregie" (1919), in *Schriften*, pp. 374–5.
31 16 January 1924.
32 Geddes, *Miracle in the Evening*, p. 296.

Bibliography in English

Bauland, Peter. *The Hooded Eagle: Modern German Drama on the New York Stage.* Syracuse, New York, 1968

Carter, Huntly. *The Theatre of Max Reinhardt.* London, 1914

Davies, Cecil W. *Theatre for the People: The Story of the Volksbühne.* Austin, Texas, 1977

Dukes, Ashley. *The Scene Is Changed.* London, 1942

Eisner, Lotte. *The Haunted Screen: Expressionism in the German Cinema and the Influence of Max Reinhardt.* London, 1969

Geddes, Norman Bel. *Miracle in the Evening: An Autobiography,* ed. William Kelley. New York, 1960

Granville-Barker, Harley. "Two German theatres," *Fortnightly Review,* 89 (London, January 1911), pp. 60–70

Hofmannsthal, Hugo von. *Selected Plays and Libretti,* ed. with introduction by Michael Hamburger. New York, 1963

Jackson, Allan S. "The Max Reinhardt Archive, New York," *Theatre Studies 20,* Columbus, Ohio, 1973–4

Martin-Harvey, John. *Autobiography.* London, 1933

Max Reinhardt Workshop of Stage, Screen and Radio in Hollywood, The (prospectus). Los Angeles, 1938

Purdom, C. B. *Harley Granville-Barker, Man of the Theatre, Dramatist and Scholar.* London, 1955

Reinhardt, Gottfried. *The Genius: A Memoir of Max Reinhardt by His Son.* New York, 1979

Sayler, Oliver M., ed. *Max Reinhardt and His Theatre.* New York, 1924; reprinted 1968 (includes *Regiebuch* for *The Miracle,* New York, 1924)

Stern, Ernst. *My Life, My Stage,* trans. Edward Fitzgerald. London, 1951

Theatre Research, vol. 5, no. 3, ed. Hans Knudsen. London, 1963

Theatre Survey, vol. 13, no. 1a. Pittsburgh, Fall 1972

Weisgal, Meyer. *So Far: An Autobiography.* New York, 1971

Wellwarth, George E. and Brooks, Alfred G., eds. *Max Reinhardt, 1873–1973: A Centennial Festschrift.* Binghamton, New York, 1973

Selected bibliography in German
(full bibliographies may be found in Braulich and Fiedler)

MISCELLANEOUS WRITING AND SPEECHES BY REINHARDT

Fetting, Hugo, ed. *Max Reinhardt Schriften: Briefe, Reden, Aufsätze, Interviews, Gespräche, Auszüge aus Regiebüchern.* Berlin, 1974

Hadamowsky, Franz, ed. *Max Reinhardt: Ausgewählte Briefe, Reden, Schriften und Szenen aus Regiebüchern.* Vienna, 1963

REGIEBÜCHER IN PRINT

Goethe. *Faust I: Passow,* Wilfried. *Max Reinhardts Regiebuch zu Faust I.* 2 vols., Munich, 1971 (dissertation)

Hofmannsthal. *Ariadne auf Naxos* (opera by Richard Strauss): *Regiebuch*. Berlin–Paris, 1912–13
Hofmannsthal. *Jedermann: Das Spiel vom Sterben des reichen Mannes und Max Reinhardts Inszenierungen*. Frankfurt-on-Main, 1973
Shakespeare. *Macbeth*: Grossmann, Manfred, ed. *Max Reinhardts Regiebuch zu Macbeth (1916), Schweize Theater Jahrbuch 31 and 32*. Basle, 1965–6
Vollmoeller. *The Miracle*: see Sayler, above

BIOGRAPHY, CRITICISM, ETC.

Adler, Gusti. *Max Reinhardt. Sein Leben*. Salzburg, 1964 (biography by Reinhardt's secretary)
Braulich, Heinrich. *Max Reinhardt, Theater zwischen Traum und Wirklichkeit*. Berlin, 1969 (a Marxist interpretation)
Fiedler, Leonhard M. *Max Reinhardt in Selbstzeugnissen und Bilddokumenten*, Hamburg, 1975 (short biography)
  Max Reinhardt und Molière. Salzburg, 1972 (short accounts of the Molière productions)
Fleischmann, Benno. *Max Reinhardt. Die Wiedererweckung des Barocktheaters*. Vienna, 1948 (chiefly on the Vienna and Salzburg years)
Hadamowsky, Franz. *Reinhardt und Salzburg*. Salzburg, 1964 (well illustrated)
Herald, Heinz. *Max Reinhardt. Bildnis eines Theatermannes*. Hamburg, 1953 (an account by Reinhardt's literary adviser)
Hollaender, Felix, Kahane, Arthur, eds. *Blätter des Deutschen Theaters*. Berlin, 1911–27 (papers published by the Deutsches Theater)
Ihering, Herbert. *Reinhardt, Jessner, Piscator oder Klassikertod?* Berlin, 1929 (essay on certain productions)
  Von Reinhardt bis Brecht, 3 vols. Berlin, 1961 (reviews)
Jacobsohn, Siegfried. *Max Reinhardt*. Berlin, 1921 (reviews)
Kahane, Arthur. *Tagebuch des Dramaturgen*. Berlin, 1928 (by Reinhardt's literary adviser)
Klingenbeck, Fritz, ed. *Max Reinhardts Theater in der Josefstadt*. Salzburg, 1972
Kvam, Kela. *Max Reinhardt og Strindbergs visionaere dramatik*. Copenhagen, 1974 (on Ibsen's *Ghosts* and the Strindberg productions, in Swedish)
Leisler, Edda and Prossnitz, Gisela, eds. *Max Reinhardt in Amerika*. Salzburg, 1976 (with details of the last years)
  Max Reinhardt in Europa. Salzburg, 1973 (essays on Reinhardt's work in different countries)
  Max Reinhardt und die Welt des Commedia dell'arte. Salzburg, 1970 (especially on *The Servant of Two Masters* and *The Salzburg Great Theatre of the World*)
  (All these books are from the Salzburg Max-Reinhardt-Forschungsstätte)
Melchinger, Siegfried, ed. *Max Reinhardt: Sein Theater in Bildern*. Hanover, 1968 (another handsome book from the Salzburg Institute)
Rothe, Hans, ed. *Max Reinhardt: 25 Jahre Deutsches Theater*. Munich, 1930 (chapters by Kahane, Herald, et al.; excellent photographs)
Stern, Ernst, *Bühnenbildner bei Max Reinhardt*. Berlin, 1955 (reminiscences)
  and Herald, Heinz, eds. *Reinhardt und seine Bühne. Bilder von der Arbeit des Deutschen Theaters*. Berlin, 1918 (with extracts from the *Regiebücher* for *A Midsummer Night's Dream, Othello, Danton's Death* and *The Miracle*)
Thimig-Reinhardt, Helene. *Wie Max Reinhardt lebte*. Percha, 1973 (autobiography by Reinhardt's second wife)

Index